AN ARAN KEENING

*For Diana, Gail and James*

*An Aran Keening*

ANDREW MCNEILLIE

THE LILLIPUT PRESS
DUBLIN

120.254.
£16.93

First published 2001 by
THE LILLIPUT PRESS LTD
62–63 Sitric Road, Arbour Hill,
Dublin 7, Ireland
www.lilliputpress.ie

A CIP record for this title is available from
The British Library.

1 3 5 7 9 10 8 6 4 2

ISBN 1 901866 63 7

*The Lilliput Press receives financial assistance
from An Chomhairle Ealaíon / The Arts Council of Ireland.*

Set in Adobe Caslon
Printed by MPG Books, Bodmin, Cornwall, England

# Contents

*Only that which aspires to a* caoin, *an edge like it*
*Like a melody tends to the infinite.*
'In Memoriam: Liam Mac 'Ille Iosa'
HUGH MACDIARMID


*'Tis true, I sometimes made a shift to catch a rabbit.*
'A Voyage to the Country of the Houyhnhnms'
JONATHAN SWIFT

## Acknowledgments

This story was finally written up for my children, as a warning shot, as they passed through their adolescence. I want to thank them for encouraging me to polish it up and polish it off. Others have encouraged me too, and they know well who they are, home and abroad. But the clearest debt I owe in seeing this book into print must go to Terence Brown, who first saw it had the makings, and next to Antony Farrell, publisher extraordinaire, and then to my compatriot Jonathan Williams. My editor Brendan Barrington tamed all wilfulness from my pen with the lightest of touches and sharpest of minds, and I'm much beholden to him.

Two of the poems here were previously published: 'They so rarely reach here now' as 'Greylags' in *Brangle*, and 'Riddle' as 'Corncrake', by the Sycamore Press; both appear in *Nevermore* (Carcanet, 2000).

# Preface

This story, this elegy and adventure, is an invention, a remembering of my stay on Inishmore from November 1968 to the early autumn of the following year. That was seventy years after the Irish playwright and poet J.M. Synge first visited the Aran Islands. Now I'm completing it in the centenary summer of Synge's auspicious visit. Based on incidents and episodes I witnessed or heard told, it begins with an account of my first, exploratory trip to Inishmore, and resumes three years later with my journey back to settle there.

Even in 1898 Synge found Inishmore too touched by capital, too tainted by the filthy modern tide, detecting in eye and expression 'the anxiety of men who are eager for gain', and even in its children 'an indefinable modern quality'. He sought his romantic, unfallen vision on Inishmaan, least accessible of the three islands, in brief visits in summer and early autumn. I didn't have such qualms when I embarked on my sea-pastoral adventure. The circumstances on Inishmore were ideal enough for me. But clearly I lived in some state deeper than I knew of resistance to the modern world. It was, after all, the 1960s, and what else was my disaffection about? For surely I went from the world as much as to the dream?

As is the inevitable nature of such things, none of the characters involved in this story, including myself, is anything other than a partial portrait, a mix of fact and fiction. To enhance disguise, elements of different individuals are compounded in my characters and transposed one with another. But I've not at any point set out to manufacture incidents or generate encounters or exchanges that did not in fact occur, in one combination or another. Nor does what follows here purport to be a documentary, encompassing the island's culture and history. Others more scholarly have abundantly furnished that need. My concern has been merely to celebrate and elegize the Aran I knew, to recount my adventures, such as they were, and recreate as best I can the world in which they passed. (I use the Anglicized place-name spellings that existed then, though I applaud the later work to retrieve their true forms.)

Also, and not too obtrusively, I hope, I've been interested to ponder my earlier self, that playboy who voyaged under my name. 'Is it me?' as Christy Mahon asks in Synge's play. 'Is it me?' No, it wasn't. Yes, it isn't. 'Kill the author!' cried the theatre crowd in Gaelic. But nowadays we know I'm dead already, an empty sack before I start. Almost every plank of my vessel has been replaced since I first crossed Galway Bay. I only truly recognize my youthful predecessor by his log, and something perhaps about the cut of his jib, a not discommendable obstinacy, as the poet said. I don't deny that I still sometimes catch myself resembling him more fully, star-gazing or map-browsing, or just delaying too long before the fishmonger's slab and fancying I can taste the salt-and-iodine, the mineral sea, and even hear it surge beneath a cloud of harrying herring gulls at the dead centre of England.

Could I now meet myself in a time-warp thirty years ago on Liverpool dock with my trunk and bags, my desert-island kit with its Shakespeare and company but no bible (Ecclesiastes and Job would doubtless have been my most thumbed books) and no 'gramophone' records (but a transistor that would corrode and die), that late October night all set for Inishmore, what would I do? I'm sure I'd rest a skinny hand upon my arm and, like the Ancient Mariner, detain myself with the stories that follow here. By middle age we're mostly grown too cautious, and selfish love for others renders us afraid. I suppose I'd argue to my earlier self that the undertaking was recklessly unwise, or urge at least postponement to a fairer time of year. I could protest with reason that his deeds would afterwards become a cross for me to bear, an albatross about my neck, a warning bell in my *curriculum vitae* suggesting submerged perils to employers. (I'd already suffered his aborted year of beer-consumption studies in the school of wild talk at a northern university.) But he lived in an age when young people cared little for CVs, if they'd ever heard of them. He stood inconceivably far from the post-Thatcherian *enfants terribles* who begin to document their achievements at the age of three. You know the type. We're all at their mercy still. But why October, almost November? Why not delay? What was there to lose? In spring the Atlantic raging less becomes approachable on foot. The cuckoo calls to the ocean, and the corncrake, with his relentless ratchet, winds back the stars: *crex crex crex crex crex crex crex crex crex crex crex crex crex* ... until you'd sell your soul for five minutes' sleep; but what price that against what imprisoning winter brings? 'Look twice, think twice, before you leap,' I suppose I'd have cautioned, 'don't be a fool.' But such is the nature of time and space we could not meet. And such is the nature of folly that it knows best. What would he have said as he kept a weather eye on the Liver Building clock, shining there like a mirrored moon that night? I'd sooner be dead? For no doubt there was a self-destructive element in this too, a death-wish in the offing. Or perhaps he'd say he went so that one day I could write this. He might claim he was generously investing in me, his future ghost-writer, my past ghost. And it's true he had his head full of stuff I'd give my eye teeth for now as I begin. Some he has bequeathed me in a little black journal (poorly bound and now disintegrating, posing some minor problems of sequence and chronology) and a bundle of letters home to his girlfriend (now my wife). The rest he entrusted in ten chapters, scribbled hard on his return, to an attic box, whence I have now retrieved them. These chart my way as I set out upon this other, belated verbal voyage, for which foresight forearms me no more than it forearmed him. The first of them is just a simple prelude, once upon a time ...

AN ARAN KEENING

I

*Once Upon a Time*

If I hadn't read J.M. Synge's little book *The Aran Islands* my life would make a different story. I say 'read', but in a strange way the book, which happened to be on our shelf in a 1912 Maunsel Roberts edition, so affected me as a youth that its pages forced me back on myself and made me dream. So I 'read' rather as Synge heard the islanders speaking Gaelic through the broken panes, or as I always fancied through the floorboards, of his lodgings, indistinctly. I had one eye on the poet and the other up the chimney, looking at the stars. This is as good a way to read as any, especially when you are young and the world first excites your conscious wonder.

My adolescence was waxing at that time and came hand in hand with an addiction to language, glutinous grammar, sinuous sentences, and the physicality of the material word. I got caught like an insect in the sticky web of words, as spun by the poets and poetic writers. Whatever they addressed, but especially if they

[ 3 ]

wrote about nature and the out-of-doors, they got the better of me. They seem to have got the better of me forever. But nothing between birth and death starts or ends at once and I still clung hard to boyish pastimes then, activities themselves that made Aran seem all the more attractive as a dream-realm. I was an ardent fisherman, and fishing is a pursuit for mystics. I was addicted obsessively to pier-haunting for whiting, rock-haunting for mackerel, surf-haunting for bass, nightlining the estuary for whatever luck would bring, or aboard the local fishmonger Mr Arundale's *What-Ho!* trawling for pram-frames, sand-logged wellingtons, barnacled cobbles, plimsolls and glistening locks of weed, with here and there a thornback skate, a box of plaice or flounder flexing, a stone or two of dogfish to rasp our dab hands, as we rode the night-tide home, over creaking mussel beds, piped ashore by waders, cold and cut from skinning skate beneath the moon and stars.

A book may have undone me and poets brought me down, but to be bespectacled by books has never been sufficient unto the day thereof for me. Much study is a weariness of the flesh, I remember reading. And so the end of my eighteenth summer saw me at Holyhead, with my holiday wages in my pocket, on the rocky road to Galway from my native Wales, intent on following the wake of J.M. Synge, to visit Aran.

I was youthful for my years and in company I was shy, too shy for my own good. Perhaps it was this that made the landlady in Galway advise me as she did. I remember as if it was yesterday her warning, just as I remember how much her words surprised me when in innocence I told her where I was bound.

'For the day is it?' she enquired sharply.

My plan was to stay for two or three days, I said, at which she exclaimed, 'Lord help us, and do you know anybody out there?' I admitted I didn't. 'Then you'd best not be going.' There was no doubt in her mind. ''Twouldn't be safe for a young fella like yourself all on his own.' She rearranged the place-setting opposite mine. The room was otherwise empty. I looked at my watch and began to poke at my breakfast.

'Aren't they wild people out there?' she began to reason. 'To be sure, some of them has never been as far as Galway in their lives, would you believe? And that's the best of them.'

I laughed and said how wise they seemed and even made her smile. She was a woman not yet of middle age, no sour old biddy, and had her wits about her.

'It's true, I'm telling you, I'm not joking,' she protested, and when she spoke next it was with scorn. 'Never out of it since they were born, can you believe? They're not fit ... not fit at all. They're ...' she seemed to search for the word, '*savages.*'

On that high moment she went tut-tutting back to the kitchen. I suppose I should have asked her why she spoke as she did, what experience had befallen her? Had it concerned a lodger? Had it, more seductively, involved a lover? Or was it merely a matter of local lore and prejudice regarding the demonized neighbour? As I left she came to the door with me and repeated her warnings as I stepped into the street.

At nine o'clock that morning the MS *Galway*, an old tub that had served as a tender to ocean-going liners, left harbour for Kilronan, Inishmore, thronged with tourists, among whom an American film crew struggled with its gear. I threaded my way to the bow, to keep lookout like Ahab until the leviathan of my obsession rose above the horizon. The film crew, having shot the view from the stern, now worked their way towards me and, thinking I might complete their picture, asked me if I'd mind turning a little this way, and a little that way, and I obliged them, this way and that way. I hardly imagined that two years later, when I was working as a news reporter in the South Wales mining town of Ammanford, half the populace, as it seemed, all in a morning, would stop to inform me of my thirty-second stardom currently to be seen at the local fleapit. I took a seat in the stalls myself that night, and the dream-like experience of seeing my image bound for Aran, floating by to an appropriately 'Celtic' soundtrack, gave a predictable spur to my longer-term intentions.

But for the time being then it was back to weddings and obituaries, and for the time being now, on this my voyage of discovery, it was September and the weather was that morning soft and sunlit. We made easy progress down the bay. Once the scene of violent fishery wars between the islanders and the netsmen of the Claddagh and often the scene of wild storms, it was now almost pacific, with just a little surge and chop and roll of breakers. Gannets plunged. Mackerel, I imagined, would somewhere be throwing themselves blind upon the hook and lobsters stumbling into pots, drunk as late bees. A brown-sailed hooker – it must have been one of the last of the old fishing craft restored – the kind of vessel that Synge sailed in more than sixty years earlier, tacked out from Connemara. The islands themselves, even as we passed Black Head on the Clare coast, remained hidden from sight in light sea-fog and cloud. But gradually three of the heavier pieces of cloud began to settle upon the sea and the islands darkened into sight. People called to each other and crowded the rail, shielding their eyes to see through the glare of sea and sky. Now with a disproportionate suddenness, and then again, as the steamer turned a degree or two north-west, with an equally drawn-out delay, and a slight wallowing and rushing of waves, before we made further perceptible advance, shields of green and badges of white settlement sharpened against the rock. The sea is the serenest dream element, when it is not a nightmare, and involuntarily as I peered ahead through the haze I remember I felt unsteady and put out a hand to grasp the rail, as you might in a dream of stepping off the kerb or more profoundly overboard, to keep my feet firm upon the deck. It was a queer momentary displacement, like being drunk. Plumes of spray snorted from the blowholes by Gregory's Sound, insisting upon the obvious resemblance of the island to a massive whale. But to me the leaping spray seemed like externalized whoops of pleasure.

How next I'd fare, among the landlady's *savages*, I would now discover as we crossed the bar and sidled towards Kilronan's harbour wall. A reception committee of jarveys hailed us, waving and pointing with their whips, to catch and hold the eye of potential passengers. I soon found myself contracted to someone below who kept pace with me along the quayside, elbowing his way among his jostling fellows, stepping over ropes, as the holiday crowd edged towards the gangway. This was Gregory, who would become my closest friend upon the island. You might mistake him, in his best jacket and cap, for a Welsh hillfarmer down to market. (There was nothing more *savage* about him, and nothing less.) The event was indeed not unlike an agricultural market or fair. The tourists went down the gangway like sheep and the islandmen, many of them tall, ranging men of the square-backed

Connacht cut, a few of them in traditional homespuns, gathered those for whom they had bid, with a nod and a wink, to offer day-trippers rides and longer-term visitors, of which at this time of year there were few, the promise of accommodation.

Gregory led me, and a young American couple, down the quay to where his horse and side-car stood. He was parked first in a long line of rigs on the road that leads back to Kilronan, the crooked little hillside metropolis of the islands, which glinted and squinted that morning in the autumn sun. Shy and impatient by nature, Gregory never had much time for this sort of work. It didn't suit him to play the courier to a party of Yanks or other pilgrims. But at the close of the season his mother welcomed all the recruits her son could press for lunch or tea or bed and breakfast. So today he'd harnessed the Big Fella and beat away down the morning air to Kilronan, on the off chance of succeeding in the competition for a passenger or two.

At the height of the season there was no want of this sort of business, if the weather would permit a sailing. Now and in the early part of the year matters were different. A man might bowl down the island and end up with nothing but a rig as empty as the unladen steamer. It was a gamble that could leave a vacuum in the heart and a thirst for consolation. So likely as not he'd end up at McDonough's or Conneely's American or Kenny's for a drop of something. Who knows but the day might then wear on until the day was forgotten, *in guinness veritas*. Then it would be all up. There'd be the horse thirsty and irritable from standing in the shafts half the day, and the cow bursting to be milked. So home he'd go, standing to drive like a charioteer, hell for leather into the quickening Atlantic night, a terror to the landladies of

Galway, could they but behold him and hear the apocalyptic clatter of his progress. Nor would home be the end of it, but he must then go out under the drunken stars – how high they are! – to negotiate the stones of the field and stalk the cow.

But Gregory would not be in such shoes this day, though the temptation to try on a similar, celebratory pair after the steamer's departure might yet prove to be his Achilles heel. Nor was he a regular drinking man but merely a man of extremes, in a place where extremity of matter and of mind, at the edge of the world, go hand in hand. He already had today thirty shillings in his pocket (ten shillings being the lower rate for five or six miles of island road in those days) and he urged us hastily aboard, wheeled the horse round, and mounted. We lunged and jolted and swayed along beneath McDonough's tall, paradoxically sober window, round the tight corner by Conneely's and on up the hill, past Kenny's and the little fire pump in its sentry box, our driver turning occasionally to glance over his shoulder and see where the rest of the field lay. But they were nowhere, only the faintest ringing of hooves below, as we plodded ahead up the great shoulder of the island.

A side- or jaunting car is the ideal vehicle for sightseeing. Perched upon it, you are high above the road and can look round and take in all points of the compass without discomfort or alarm, once you get used to the way it can pitch and swing at a corner or slope upon a hill. The sea now filled more and more of the eye. Behind us Inishmaan emerged to view, dark and distant in a widening moat. To the north lay the coast of Connemara and far upon the horizon the Twelve Pins, to the east the cliffs of Moher. It was day of soft warm air and haze, a Siren day of wheeling choughs, *kazoo-kazoo*, and ravens lunging, *cronk-cronk*, in which all hope for me, if ever hope had been, was lost. We reached the level. Gregory looked along the grey road as if along the barrel of a gun and with a calculated shot of his whip fired the Big Fella about his business.

Until now there had been little or no talk between us. What there had been concerned mere practicalities of destination and accommodation. But at last even the reluctant and reticent Gregory felt compelled to expand and fell into sporadic conversation with the American couple who sat on the opposite side of the car to mine.

'Were you ever in Aran before?' I heard him begin in the nasal and elusive English of the islands.

'I've been to Donegal,' said the man behind me, having mistaken 'Aran' for 'Ireland'. To which Gregory responded, dismissively, and with a befitting circularity, 'Ah Donegal is in Donegal, but *Aran* is Aran.'

I left them to it, to the indeterminacy of translation, and sank into solipsistic wonder at the view in general, and at the rocks to either side in particular, the terraces of limestone paving, fissured, ragged, jagged, mapped with lichen and honeycombed with dry-stone walls that as often as not enclosed nothing but stone and light. ('The walls is where we put the stones,' Gregory once mocked to me, 'when we were looking for the earth.') It is a commonplace that Aran, like much of Connemara, has little or no topsoil and that the people created what soil there is by accumulations of seaweed and sand. Here and there you saw a pocket of green or a garden of potatoes, their haulms down now and bedrock visible between the rows, or, more rare, a bleaching shock of rye, brimming the walls like creamy milk in a bowl. This was rye left to luck, in the hope that it would ripen for seed and grow long enough for thatch straw. Some walls enclosed live-stock: a pair of goats with linked collars, so that when one looked up to see us pass the other must look up too, and now and then cattle, sheep, a horse, an ass braying to the barren rocks (such a thing in the desert to hear the wild ass bray). A desolate square house or two stood pitched above the road and down on the ter-race below were picture-postcard cabins. We sped on down the long hill from Oatquarter, passing a grey stone crucifix, stark against the Atlantic skyline, in a little walled area by the road, and entered what passes for the Eden of Inishmore, the plain of Kil-murvey, with its foursquare 'big house', its thumbnail of silver sand, its several broad fields and its ancient clifftop fort, Dún Aengus (Bronze Age, Aengus the Gaelic for Aeneas), startling, at the very sheer edge of Europe. Gregory pointed out the land-marks, but what I remembered in the intervening years before my legendary sojourn, to which this account is merely the prelude, was the intoxicating air, full of the sea that drawled and crumped and hushed on the sand, and the ancient tattoo of hoofbeats, tap-ping as we clipped along the road behind the dunes. It was a site that in the distant past had been the scene of a desperate battle, and the ground beneath the relatively new roadway had on exca-vation yielded many human skulls.

To reach the village of Kil-na-cer, when coming from the east, you take the turning below the graveyard and travel on through Kilmurvey. Instead of turning right at the ball alley you go on ahead, down the narrow track, which swings slowly left and begins to crowd with overhanging fuchsia. There around the corner, as if set to spy across the way upon the dozen and a half denizens of Kilmurvey, you come upon the original settlement of close-set cabins, narrow lanes and paths amid high-walled gardens, that was once Kil-na-cer. At that time only two of the old dwellings were inhabited. Others stood empty, complete with everything – dressers of cobwebbed china, milk jugs in rows, dinner plates, cups hanging on hooks, saucepans, kettles (burial urns for spiders), empty wardrobes, beds and musty mattresses – everything but tenants. On others, fallen tiles and crumbled mortar let the weather in. Drab, weather-blackened thatch hung torn or had fallen away. Roofless homes sat knee-deep in weeds, chimney-breasts bared, the haunts of cats, and of fowl that looked to nest away. All were prey to the evictions of those extortionate landlords, poverty and time, from which the present village had attempted to dissociate itself by moving on a few yards. It comprised four houses, a modern bungalow, and three outhouses of undressed stone, in a group at the lane end.

No one stirred out at the sound of the horse, and this reminded me that we'd seen no one on the road or anywhere else since we left Kilronan. Where was everyone? Drawn to the steamer at Kilronan or in New York or Boston or on some English motorway or a building site in London. Nurse, night-watchman, labourer, I would know of three at least. But probably someone left behind turned to a window, looked and looked away again, or glanced through a half-open door or above a wall top, for there might be something in it. But there was nothing, only the last of the season's visitors. For winter stood around the corner, or at least that change in the Atlantic weather that heralded winter.

Gregory halted us at a little wicket gate in a wall that was unusually backed by a sparse hedge of suburban privet (I remember it particularly because one day it figured in an odd incident between us) and beyond which stood his mother's house. We climbed down and he started to turn the horse but something troubled it. It flattened its ears, began to snort and to back the car at the wall.

'Stand clear,' called Gregory. 'Stand clear, I said.'

He shouted fiercely, as if apportioning blame to his passengers, and he cursed the horse as it reared and wheeled back, this side and that, grazing the varnished car against the wall, dislodging a boulder. His cap fell in the road before he could catch the curb chain and draw the horse down, and now cursing and hot he snatched it up, tugged it on and led the rig back down the lane. I turned to follow the Americans up the path to the house. Gregory's mother, having heard the rumpus, was coming busily down, wiping her hands on her apron.

'Well, I don't know,' she said, smiling and tutting, 'poor Sonny.'

'Kinda mean horse,' said the American woman.

'Ah,' said the old lady, 'never trust a horse.'


To avoid my fellow tourists I had been scrambling along the low shore all that first afternoon, exploring westwards, prospecting as if I'd already made my mind up, inspecting likely fishing spots, postponing the temptation of the high cliffs, when late in the evening I climbed back on to the road towards Kilmurvey, thinking to cut up to the old fort before nightfall and see the clifftop view. I came upon a man leaning on the sea-wall by the bay. He

turned as I approached, as if he knew by a sixth sense I was coming and only awaited my arrival. A burly, close-cropped man he
was, with thick forearms and eyes that almost closed as he smiled
his greeting.

'Hello, there,' he called affably, and then turned back to look
at the bay where a curragh rode, or, as the islanders say, 'swam',
light as a feather at a mooring. He dandled a pick-axe handle and
let it swing slowly like a pendulum, to and fro. It knocked against
the wall occasionally and made a resounding *chock, chock* as it hit.

'The weather is on the turn, I'd say. Summer's gone.'

I agreed that it had been a beautiful day and leant against the
wall beside him.

'I'll not be long after it either, thank God,' he continued. 'Isn't
it a terrible place and no mistake?' He didn't look for an answer.
'But you wouldn't know. You're just off the boat this morning?' I
said I was. 'Four months,' he resumed, 'four months I've done
sticking up telegraph poles, and only twice been into Galway.' He
shot me a confiding glance. 'They're terrible savages here, you
know.'

I thought at once of the landlady in Galway. It seemed she
had a cousin.

'I've heard say, but ...'

'But nothing,' he laughed. 'The most ignorant backward savages in all Ireland, and that's saying something, believe me.
That's one you won't find in the Guinness Book of Records, but
it's a fact.'

We spoke a little about where we came from and so on (he
was a Kerry man) and then he pushed himself up off his elbows
and stood ready to go.

'And mind,' he advised, 'mind, if you have any trouble while you're here, be sure to come and see me. I'm staying up the road at Kil-na-cer.'

With this he raised the pick-axe handle, stabbed the air before him with its broad head, and swung it up onto his shoulder, with a deftness that indicated great suppleness of wrist and just the suggestion, perhaps, of a previous incarnation as a military policeman.

'Goodbye, now, and good luck.'

'Goodbye,' I said, and, not knowing then the name of the village I was staying at, I didn't think I'd meet the man again, unless it be upon the road. And so we regarded each other with some surprise as I came in for my supper, and even some embarrassment, as old Mrs Feaney, than whom no one could be more civil or less savage, introduced us. The engineer's conversation was now appropriately diplomatic and we talked about the telephone and how he'd worked that summer with island labour to bring the line out to the west of Inishmore.

By nightfall a heavy canopy of cloud hung over the island. There it loomed all the next day, a great dome of luminous grey, amplifying the slightest sound – the wren's voice in the ivy, the small surf, the muted boom of the Atlantic, the beat of hooves upon a distant road, the bark of dogs between villages. It played tricks with the light, rinsing all colours, finding indigos and heather purples, ochres, rust and coal black in the grey rock, and drew imaginary lines of rain across the window. How could it not have rained? The fishing boats looked black against a sheared-lead sea. The ocean was as calm as it could ever be. (Tomorrow it would send a spume of spray two hundred feet and more into the air. You'd see it from the Feaneys' kitchen window, shooting above the cliffs, at least a quarter of a mile away.)

At some – at most – perspectives, because the walls are high and the areas they encompass small, the island looks as if it is composed of nothing but rock. It lies in the ocean like the petrified hulk of a giant ship, battleship grey, blackened, rusting, its queer camouflage fading. That second day I walked down the island, scrambling over boulders, clambering over walls, to the south and east, amid the crazy geometry of slab and boulder. Coming up to one wall above the sea and beginning to climb it, I nearly fell off backwards as a tall skinny man sprang up, equally startled, and stared at me from the other side. He laughed as I addressed him and shook his head, and laughed all over his face, as he tried very brokenly to indicate that he did not understand English. I could not see what business he was engaged in, there above the sea. The field he stood in was empty and he carried nothing with him. His sweater was all but threadbare about the neck, shoulders, elbows and cuffs. He seemed oblivious of all appearance.

At Kilronan I stopped for a Guinness at Kenny's mahogany-dark, fire-lit bar and heard above the solemn silence of early-evening drink and cards one islander say to another, to entertain some tourists in his company, 'Every day is a holiday on Aran. That's how it is here now. That kind of way.' And indeed, as I would discover, that's how it was for some, a holiday. For others, it was a prison sentence.

It began to rain in the night and rained steadily for a few hours, loud enough to disturb your sleep, and a wind gathered with the dawn and by early morning went howling at every door.

Gregory and his brother Bartley, who lived just on the outskirts of the village, took advantage of the bad weather to give each other 'a clip', as their mother said, and they occupied the kitchen, joking and protesting as the one cropped the other's hair to the bone with a cumbersome pair of scissors and a great metal comb. The rain rattled on window and door and showed no sign that it would stop, so I decided to go out, encouraged by Mrs Feaney's observation that rain is 'healthy', on a quest to reach the far west, to see Bungowla. Bungowla, where stands the Black Rock of Woe, is or was a small settlement of cabins, right at the bottom of the hill, in a turmoil of rocks, just above a pair of loughs, overlooking the strait between Inishmore and the Brannock Islands (or Brannogues – where I'd later have adventures).

It was late by the time I made it back to the village and I was soaked, without a dry stitch on my body, though drier for the long walk back along the cliffs to Dún Aengus. Wouldn't I change and put my wet clothes next the range? Wouldn't I sit and have a cup of cocoa before bed? So we sat by the range, while my clothes steamed, Gregory uncapped and in his stockinged feet, his mother tutting on about the death of cold I'd catch. The other guests returned – some merrily from the pub – and filed through the kitchen to light their candles and mount the stairs. I felt distinguished not to be among them, and to be sitting by the hearth, especially as the engineer rolled up and passed ungreeted, and to share their talk about the weather and the work Gregory had now before him, harvesting the spuds, and how old Mrs Feaney had earlier that year returned from New York where she had visited her son. She had flown from Shannon and they had seen Aran below. The recollection seemed to render her all but speechless and she smiled embarrassedly and shook her head as if the matter lay far beyond words, somewhere across a gulf of feeling as wide as the Atlantic.

The Feaneys urged me now not to delay my stay beyond the next boat for the weather had become 'cranky', as old Mrs Feaney put it (I would later hear her use the word to excuse her daughter Mary's winter moods), and I could get stranded for who knew how long. So I took their advice and, after one more day of explorations, Gregory drove me without charge, dismissing my repeated efforts to press ten shillings in his hand, to catch the boat. I carried in my bag for souvenirs a stone the size of a decent potato and a succulent plant from Mrs Feaney. She had disappeared to pick it at the last minute round the back of the house from the guttering of an old building, while Gregory waited impatiently in the lane. As she gave it to me, to bring good fortune to my house, and as we stood on the garden path, she pressed my hand and said, 'God bless you and save you, sir,' and prompted by what I could not tell she confided as I took the plant, 'You are more like us than the others,' and nodded towards the lane where the others, poor creatures, sat upon the car inspecting their watches and worrying if they wouldn't miss the boat.

## 2

## *The Eye of the Storm*

Three years passed and found me with a bigger hoard of wages,
big enough, I thought, to see me through a year of island life. My
elsewhere was so well rooted in my mind that nothing could sup-
plant it, not even my new girlfriend. I was obsessed. Each night
I made an appointment with the shipping forecast. When Shannon surfaced, Rockall and Malin Head, and all those resonant
names since immortalized by Seamus Heaney, like Finistère and
Bloody Foreland, bespeaking the ends of the earth, I'd lie there
dreaming in my lodgings of how the night might be about the
islands. A furnace of stars, I imagined, or a black mare galloping,
the moon in her mane. The islanders would be tucked up abed.
Rocked to sleep by the Atlantic, they'd be dreaming of eligible
partners. Or Morpheus's perfect postman would deliver to their
bedsides letters from America abulge with news and dollars. Or
else at sea, fishing in the bay, they'd hear the very words I heard.
There was something rousing in the thought of their spare lives

among the waves, at the margin of the airwaves, and this inspired me and filled me with longing to escape. I read whenever I could books of the sea and wilderness (call me Ishmael), and poems, and dreamt of my imminent pursuit along the pathway to experience. Nothing would keep me from my purpose. In the end I went headlong.

Had I only troubled to enquire before lugging my trunk, suitcase and bags from Euston to Galway (any sensible person would have sent the trunk on ahead), I would at least have known that the steamer, the *Naomh Eanna*, had made her last voyage to the islands until Christmas. The discovery knocked a little of the wind out of my philosophy. I bedded down in Galway, deliberately stealing a last taste of luxury at the suitably named Atlantic Hotel on Eyre Square, and hung about the town.

While the *Naomh Eanna* prepared to tack round the bum of Erin, Dublin-ward, as I was told, for a Board of Trade Survey, her place was to be taken, on 5 November, by an island trawler. The weather was so wild even the trawler would not risk a journey. The fleet was penned ashore. The islands blazed like coals in a fire. A boat was due to cross to Rossaveal, along the coast in Connemara, on Tuesday, to collect supplies and mail. Of course there was no guarantee that it would come.

The delay in my progress proved useful. It gave me time to buy in more supplies. I bought tinned food, matches, candles, a bottle of rum, some hooks and hanks of fishing line. Had I known more about freight charges, about the island's cost of living and its winter scarcities, I would have bought more. (I would have bought mouse-traps. I would have bought cheese.) As I patrolled from the quay to Lough Corrib, from the lough to the

Claddagh, the weather rattled wildly through the town, accompanied by hail and rain. Tinker girls and women huddled on corners or in shop doorways. By Naughton's and Lipton's they accosted passers-by. 'Give us a couple of coppers, sor,' called one to me, proffering a little cardboard box as if the hand were too blunt an instrument. (This was an unfamiliar sight to a young man from pre-Thatcherian Britain.) Their menfolk, intent upon more important business of an undisclosable order, clipped by occasionally at a trot on empty barrows, legs dangling, heads cocked against wind and rain. And 'Try-bune! Try-bune!' cried the raw corner-boys, touting the local rag. In the damp and billowing pages of the *Connacht Tribune* ('For Faith and Fatherland') you might learn about true wonders of the western world: the next dance at the Talk of the Town Ballroom (door prize a Connemara pony), who stole what from whom, who got six months suspended, who got married, who died of natural causes, who drowned, what vessels were calling at Galway harbour, what team won and what team lost, what price heifers (£8.5.0 the live hundredweight) …

What I could not learn, for only time could teach me, was how overwhelmingly tempting, how rich with life, how warm and welcoming, how cosy, the prospect of Galway would at times become in the months ahead – Galway, grey city of the tribes or of the thirteenth tribe, as they now said, referring to the tinker hordes that now besieged it. And this was not a feeling peculiar to a stranger softened by a sedentary trade, but a common one among the islanders. If Galway didn't exist, the islands would have invented it, for all manner of purposes and reasons.

But now my highest hope was to put the town behind me, a

*120,254.*

founding reason for its existence. The morning of the appointed day dawned dismally. As I crossed the square in search of a taxi the wind tucked the rain under my collar like a rough-handed barber and smarmed my head with rain as thick as oil. It seemed improbable a crossing would be made. There was nothing to choose between Tuesday, Monday, Sunday or Saturday. If anything the weather was wilder today as we drove out than it had been any day since my arrival. But then, what hope the next day? What hope at all, I wondered, as I caught with exhilaration a fumey glimpse of the islands themselves where the road emerges and hugs the coast in a brief embrace. North Sound looked as hospitable as the fires and brimstone of hell. The taxi-driver wasn't prepared to say one way or another whether he thought my journey worth the fare, from my side of the bargain that is. In fact he wasn't prepared to say much at all. He was otherwise preoccupied by the agitations of his ulcer, and the bad back that had prevented him from helping me to heave my trunk aboard. At the edge of the town we stopped to buy a pint of milk and sat while he gasped and sweated, a bag of guts in his nylon shirt, and swilled the milk down. I suppose I was fortunate to reach Rossaveal at all.

'Here today, Connemara,' gasped the ulcer, bravely airing his much-perforated pun as I leant in and paid him. The taxi then turned sharply and sped off back through the wet to Galway. I stood abandoned in the wilderness with my box and baggage. The inlet and jetty lay a few hundred yards away, down a steep track below the road. My heart sank a little, I confess, and sank still more with a sudden ebb, as it dawned on me that the tide was out about as far as it could go. The lobster boats in the little harbour wallowed on their sides like pigs in mud. Unless the tide made rapidly, no boat could come or go for hours. But a much larger doubt concerned the open sea, whose turbulence I had witnessed from the road. The prospects of a crossing were dim, as dim as the winter light down on the jetty, beneath the grey slopes, with their rain-blackened boulders and rusting bracken. I stood on the roadside, undecided. There was no sign of habitation ahead (in fact the village stood around the corner). So I concluded that the little white bungalow at the foot of the jetty was all the settlement there was to the place called Rossaveal, which did not even figure on the map I had.

In the end I made up my mind (having come so far what choice did I have?) to trust to the promise of a crossing. So I lugged all my belongings down and stacked them under the sea wall. It took some effort manoeuvring my trunk (it wasn't as robust as it once had been and it had never been very robust, being of a cheap kind, made of light wood and fabric with reinforcing wooden bands: it was the symbol of my adventure). I progressed perhaps a foot at a time, swinging it from corner to corner, wary as it creaked and cracked that it might split on a jutting rock and spill my worldly goods into the wet. Each time I passed the bungalow I hoped someone might emerge to call me in for shelter, but no one did. No tell-tale gull sat warming on the chimney either. Nor was there, as far as I could see, so much as a twitch of inquisitive lace curtain to spy who might be coming and going. I assumed there was no one at home. So I found as much shelter as I could between a stack of lobster pots and the sea wall, and there I stood, and there I waited. The tide barely moved, nor for an hour or more did anything else, except for the cloud overhead, which careered inland, and the rain, and the odd gull skulking among the weed-draped boulders at the water's edge. Yet I felt quite unreasonably sanguine and never once did I regret or even pause to recall my former life, of just a few days earlier, at the hub of 'events'.

How much time had blown by and how many gallons of rain had been tipped over me I don't know, but at last a figure appeared on the road above, paused, and to my pleasure began the climb down. This was Michael. A resident of Kilmurvey, he was, as I would discover, the most immediately forthcoming man in the vicinity of Kil-na-cer. I was always pleased to encounter Michael because I could depend upon him for a conversation. But his melancholy talk could be depressing too, bespeaking poverty and disadvantage. As if to make the difference between our positions clear, he would almost invariably conclude our talks abruptly with, 'But you have your holidays,' and turn back to his business, of gathering seaweed or whatever it might be. Or he'd say, 'There is nothing for nothing, only the briars on the rocks and the seaweed on the strand. That's how it is here now,' and turn away. He seemed to grow impatient with himself, rather than with me, and never showed a hint of surliness or personal resentment, for which I would have excused him more than readily: for I was young and did nothing to maintain myself that he could see, and for all he knew or might be disposed to believe, I never had. Square-built, long-limbed and upright, he was difficult to age in his cap and oiler (as they call their oilskins on the island). Even in his ordinary working clothes it was hard to tell how old he was. Only when he took off his cap, say to knot a moist handkerchief round his head on a hot day, when the corn-crake ran silently before the scythe, or broke from cover in brief, skimming flight, might you begin to guess his true age and see how life had worn him. For Michael had the bald head of an elderly man, a pale old head, slightly waxen with a pressing premonition of the skull beneath the skin. Without the shelter of his otherwise habitual cap you also saw old age about, if not within, his slightly sunken eyes. He dwelt much and morbidly on death. He would one day take care to show me where in the graveyard above Kilmurvey bay his bones would lie.

But at that time, of course, I knew nothing about him and he knew nothing of me. He came straight up, nodded a greeting, set down his sack, stepped across to peer into the harbour and remarked contemptuously, 'There's not enough water there for a curragh to swim in.' 'Do you think there'll be a boat?' I asked, with the fatuity bred of fading hope, for my impatience to arrive on Aran had just begun to get the better of me. 'They'd know beyond, do you see?' He jerked a thumb at the bungalow. 'They can ring Kilronan from there and ask has any boat left.' But both being awkwardly independent, we neither of us took so much as a step towards the bungalow. Instead we leant together with our backs against the wall, watching the rain, and, in a manner of speaking, being watched by it.

Michael had been to Athenry on some errand concerning a jaunting car, a rare and momentous expedition. He'd been out of the island for a week, which he protested did not please him. (Though he always made as if he longed to leave, to hit the road to Dublin.) If the boat didn't come he'd a mind to put his bag on his back and swim home like the whale with his hump, he said. But with the patience of the falling rain he stood and softly searched me out, to know my business and where I came from.

(Yet I was no Welshman with a name like that.) He made no comment as to my 'business'. But he seemed mockingly amused when, more anxious to make conversation than to parade a hobby-horse, I explained that my name was an Anglicized spelling, itself in its precise form over five hundred years old, of the ancient Gaelic Mac an Filidh, son of the poet or poets (though a Scottish Gaelic speaker once demoted me to 'son of the servant to the poet or poets', saying 'ghillie' to himself). It belonged indeed, I expanded (maybe I did have the bit between my teeth after all), to County Antrim and the ancient kingdom of Galloway in Scotland.

Michael's surname, Gill, on the other hand, was merely an English legacy. 'I am English,' he said with a smile, 'on account of the British constabulary, I do believe, not thanks to Oliver Cromwell, as some do say.' For Cromwell had garrisoned the island and the islanders knew their history. (Cromwell of course it was who drove those Irish that he did not kill to Connacht. 'To hell or Connacht' was his phrase. It has stood the test of time.) Indeed the English ruling class had poked their clerical and con-stabular noses in on Aran right on through the nineteenth cen-tury (as J.M. Synge gives witness), as they have in Ireland even beyond the founding of the republic, blundering with their cus-tomary patrician conceit and murderous soldiery in the cause, ultimately, of barbarians like Carson and Paisley.

In the meantime the tide began stirring, sucking in and out between the stones at the foot of the jetty. Then once more the telephone surfaced and without explaining, or even acknowledg-ing, his own reluctance to enquire, Michael worked me, until I could no longer resist his importuning, to knock at the bungalow and make a call. I trudged off and rapped at the door. Just as I was about to turn away, convinced there was no one in, a deaf old lady answered. Like the actress and the bishop, it was not the first time she'd been called upon. She asked to see the colour of my coppers and kept me waiting while I dug into my pockets. Then to my surprise she let me in and I stood dripping in the hall while she wound away at the phone, sounding some bell beyond the bay in the post office at Kilronan. It took much frenzied cranking to raise an answer. Then came an exchange in Irish loud enough to have been conducted against the storm itself, from one rocky promontory to another. It did not trouble me that the conversation continued and rambled on for some time. A sweet smell of cooking churned my stomach and the warmth indoors made my face and hands tingle happily. Even I recognized briefly when I was well off. I could hear the rain driving at the door and the wind blustering.

By the time I stepped back out into the submerged morning the scene had transformed itself. Michael stood with another man, an Inishmaanite, and down the hill, with a little knot of men behind it, lumbered a great CIÉ wagon. These men had taken the bus that left Galway at midday, as I should have done. The lobster boats were up now off their elbows and swinging on their moorings. The sea ran quick and loud against the wall. I was heartened and strode smartly up to Michael, now deep in talk with the Inishmaanite. 'Two boats left Kilronan a while back,' I said with an air of importance, I suppose, such as bearers of good news often assume, as if they are not merely ciphers but engineers of fortune itself. Michael looked round, seeming to have forgotten my existence. The other man jerked his head dismissively towards the inlet and said, 'They are come now.' And so they were, riding down in single file, sliding forward on the tide, which came flooding in at speed, as if a sluice had been opened at the edge of the bay.

In no time the boats were at the quayside moored, and the vessel serving as a ferry disembarking. The activity was hectic. The incoming party, every man-jack shaken, green- and sallow-faced, told of their ordeal in terms that united the rest of us with nervous mirth. A priest, wearing a pallor as white as his collar, looked as he might have looked on prematurely meeting his maker. His black mac and trouser legs were, I noticed, flecked with breakfast (not necessarily his own) – curls of tomato skin, and gobbets like cold porridge. He vouched for the truth of every word. Things were so bad out in the bay, he said, that another trawler attempting to reach the islands from Galway had earlier that morning been driven back when almost in the lee of Inishere. But no one seemed to doubt we would set out. The fishermen worked fast as canisters of Guinness, gas bottles, tea-chests, mail bags, my trunk and all that sailed with her, were winched into the hold. A boy in the crew worked so hard that he swung the empty hook back towards the quay in an arc that all but took the skipper's head with it. For his enthusiasm he received a verbal ear-boxing so sudden and severe it seemed to silence the gale and left us all momentarily gaping.

But now we climbed aboard. Our vessel lay astern of the other trawler, which was to stay behind, holed up in this dour haven. (I believe it was the doomed boat of whose fate you will learn later.) We moved off astern while its skipper, drawing on a cigarette, leant watching us from the wheelhouse doorway. The wheelhouse of a traditional inshore trawler is more capacious than might appear from the quayside or the shore. But it is not designed to accommodate ten men and a crew of four or five. I didn't think quite what a press there would be inside, and stood on deck with my back to the housing to savour our departure and watch the white bungalow and the jetty, the brackened and rocky slopes, swim in our wake until they sank from view. After all, this was a moment of which I had often dreamed, the last leg of my voyage, the last riddance, as I thought, of mere mundanity and trivial division. So I thanked but declined Michael when solicitously he tugged my sleeve as he pushed by and pressed his way inside; I left him thinking, I suppose, that I would learn the hard way if I'd learn at all. The inlet itself was no more than choppy. I had been on worse seas off the coast of Wales aboard the *What-Ho!* Although I'd felt queasy on occasion, I'd never before been sick at sea. So I wasn't apprehensive about that, not for the time being. Nor did the sea grow rougher steadily as we advanced. It did so all at once, as we entered the open water.

Having made all fast, the crew edged their way into the wheelhouse and disappeared from view between the sardined bodies, down a well in the corner, where no one else was prepared to go, into the bowels of the boat. Down there in the dark beneath the sea, amid the stink of fish boxes, the reek of diesel, they lay, men of quite other resilience, while the engine thudded and laboured, and the boat bucked and reared and corkscrewed, tumbling off cliffs into what seemed unfathomable abysses, until the igneous sea surged up and threw out a mountain upon which we landed like an ark in a flood, rocking, the propeller in mid-air, grinding. In the inlet it was nothing. In the inlet it was easy. But, aware now that our progress would not remain so blithe, I seized the chance and used the wedge driven by the crew to find a foothold, at least, inside the wheelhouse. I stood half-in-half-out, braced against the jamb, where I could experience the best and worst of both worlds, the wild sea air and the shelter of the housing, without the absolute perils of the one or the claustrophobia of the other.

Once upon the open sea (as all the worst sea stories should begin) there was no time to relish the romance of voyaging. At first, everyone's most urgent concern was to keep upright, if only in relation to the boat, and stand his ground. So shoulder braced against shoulder, elbow against elbow (or if needs be rib), the party stood while the boat rocked and rocketed. The windscreen, swept by a long and lazy wiper that juddered ineffectually as it went, looked now at the sea, now at the heavens, but mostly at a film of brine. Brine smashed aboard and streamed shin-deep down the decks, re-swamping my already swamped outside boot with water that felt more like liquid ice. And in the wheelhouse, Adam's apples began to bob like corks on a flood; faces grew sallow; men fidgeted, adjusted their collars, felt unduly hot, removed with difficulty their caps, put them back on with even greater difficulty, and tried to outstare the inevitable. Nothing in the wide day would stand steady, unless it was at the bottom of the sea. The storm – for the wind was later recorded as being at storm force – roared and rushed and swept the wave crests to the skies. (On Inishmore it levelled entire lengths of stone wall.) We could see neither the mainland nor the islands, but only each other and the toppling sides of the sea, as the skipper tried to ride the switchback ridges home. Men who had been this way before, who could or could not swim, thought of drowning, the water round them bubbling. They wished that they were dead, or better far instead, anywhere on terra firma. One man, when first we rode into the sound, I think he must have been a schoolmaster, called out, 'Hands up all those who're doing this for fun.' I raised my outside hand but no one saw, no one could turn but a quarter turn of the head, no one inside could raise an arm, if any indeed were there unnecessarily. I raised my hand, as if to wave goodbye. Waving and not, as yet, drowning.

The first man to break and go lunging out seemed to licence a general capitulation. In ones, they broke past me, in twos they forced me out on deck, but with two or three out there I could step back inside completely. Even the boy, the one in the French beret who'd nearly decapitated the captain, bobbed up from the well. I saw him appear, suddenly, like a cormorant surfacing. He swallowed, seemed to blink, and then scuttled, as if waterlogged, for the doorway. And so as the boat careered as wildly as ever and the storm roared, men flung themselves out to be sick. They clung to whatever hatch or bar or strut they could grab and with the help of the wind and of the vessel's violently lurching motion they turned themselves wretchedly inside out, while the sea washed them down again.

The inner being in such circumstances is at the mercy of the inner ear. Michael, I noticed, did not succumb and there were perhaps two or three others, including the skipper and, barring the boy, his crew. But they must have been born to it or by repeated batterings found immunity. I took my turn quite early. The worst part of it was clinging to the vessel for your life, by whatever means you could. That concentrated the mind like nothing else and distracted you from all discomfort. One slip of the hand and you were gone, a dead man – there was nothing anyone could have done about it.

Once we made it to the lee of Inishmore, the impact of the storm diminished. We ran along less violently and, hardened by what we'd been through, began to weigh our sorrow with our comfort and to stand on deck wherever we might find a handhold, to recover our composure. As to the island, all you could see was a blackened shoreline and a smokey, billowing mass of mist. 'There it is,' said the Inishmaanite to me, 'there is your jail.' But I was too dazed yet, too dead or alive, neither fish nor man, to answer.

A boy wobbled his bicycle down the puddled quay. Either he wobbled or I had still to find my balance after the roller-coaster sea. A black and white dog tailed behind him, stopped to bark at a gull perched on the mast of a trawler, and went on its way again, tail down in the wet. The bark seemed muffled by the mist that spilt down through the village to the harbour. The gull launched itself into the mizzling evening air, sailed round and realighted. Stillness hung in the high shelter of the bay, at odds with the roaring world beyond it.

Men loitered against the wall, idly talking and watching, their eyes remote with more than shyness or November cold. What would that queer hawk there be doing here? Tuesday was dole day and the world was the busier and the fuller for it. The boat and its arrival constituted an event of some curiosity and interest, to be observed at first hand should you be remotely in the vicinity. If you had a package ordered you could speed its progress home by coming down to meet the boat yourself, and in the process you might hear news, how things had been, who was it stranded now from Inishmaan, things to connect together, food for talk. The carriers prepared to take away in an assortment of pickups and tractor-trailers the cargo we had ferried. Gone with the last tourist were the jaunting cars and other horse-drawn rigs of the summer season. Here was unaccommodating winter with a vengeance. Explosive Guinness canisters swung up to the quayside from the dark hold, catching what little light there was, as if they were pure and polished silver. I stood sobering up, the fool in his dream-days, postponing the world, like one of Dante's hawkers, no Virgil or Statius to call him away to more becoming business. I felt like a waterlogged seabird blinking his eye, or like someone who'd just surfaced from the crack at Kenny's or Conneely's American, dole-full, and drunk as November's Atlantic sky. I waited a while for my baggage to be winched ashore, and thought as I did how different was the scene that wild evening from the morning of my first visit. But this was what I had come to discover, how the islanders survived their winter, how the winter loomed in their minds. What was it like to live each day to the clock of the winter weather and the tides, in poverty and hardship?

Someone had been keeping an eye out for me. Not Gregory, for whom I'd looked among the faces by the wall, but old Mr McDonough, who had let me stand and look around while he loaded gas cylinders and other commodities into his pickup. For that was his casual, independent style. Once my trunk landed he came over with a smile to ask if I was the one for Kil-na-cer. I never knew if he'd been in America but he had the cut of a New Hampshire or Vermont farmer. In his check lumber shirt and braces he made me think of photos I'd seen of Robert Frost. I climbed aboard and off we set, slowly over the bumpy and busy quay. McDonough blew his horn at a pair of old women in black shawls and skirts who walked shoulder to shoulder back towards Kilronan. And they ignored him, holding to the middle of the road. 'Ah, sugar,' he cried, 'come on!', drumming on the steering wheel like some commuter in a traffic jam. He revved the engine up their skirts and tooted his horn. When finally, having made their point, they stepped out of the road, and we drew level with them, McDonough stopped. 'We'll give one of those a lift,' he said, and so I made to open the door. 'No, no,' he checked me firmly, 'she can ride on the back.' The poor old crone hopped aboard and off we wound into Kilronan and up the island's shoulder.

Once we reached the ridge we felt the full brunt of the wind and rain. It was like being back at sea. The old woman crouched down as close to the cab as she could and drew her shawl about her. It would be cold out there and a rocky ride on the hard metal floor of the truck among the clanking gas cylinders. It would be wet. I was unhappy about the woman's plight, but 'When in Rome ...' was a dictum I thought it wisest to observe. (First comprehend your Roman, as Mrs Beeton might have said by way of starting a hare.) What did I know? Maybe the lady was a handful? Maybe she'd drink taken? And yet I do not think so. She was Maggie Faherty and I came to know her. Her cabin lay a garden's distance from my own. She lived there with her brother Tam and her brother the Yank, and I would watch her every day, with her broom, shooing the chickens from the door, or see her shawled head bobbing beyond the wall as she struggled back from the well with her water pails. Half crazed she might have been at times, and once, as you will see, she put the finger on me for a thief, but she was kindly and benign and full of humour. I don't know what it was, unless it was her sex, or poverty (she would not have had the price of the fare). Might not such a thing be waived?

The rain flew hard and the billowing cloud rolled and smoked across the rocks. At this height and in such weather the island seemed like a mountain top in a land of geysers where steam gushed and hissed from the hot stone. It was late evening (by evening I mean afternoon, a term not used on the island), about four o'clock, and although the hour was gloomy, there were shifts in the light, and monotone subtleties. Forty shades of grey and more if you had the patience to count them. Doubtless I'd have time enough ahead for cataloguing the colour grey.

McDonough pumped me about the crossing and how had I enjoyed it. Not feeling much inclined to talk, for I'd still not recovered my spirits from the sea, I put the worst face on it that I could, compatible with not losing face. He was a sharp and a shrewd little man for all his smiles and twinkling gaze, and no one could call him a slouch at business. At any rate, he lined me up for three gas cylinders before I knew I'd have need of them. And then, quicker than you could strike a match, he sold me a gas fire too. He knew the place I was to rent, which was more than I did, and said it would be cold and damp, with only the kitchen hearth, and I would need a fire to warm my bedroom. There was a mantle lamp and a little gas stove with two burners. McDonough rattled on but then stopped talking at once, and, with a kind of awkward reverence you might say, lurched us sharply, almost belatedly, to the right, with a rattle and clatter and who knows what for the old woman in the back, as we came down through Oatquarter, to avoid a woman in a headscarf who knelt motionless in prayer before the roadside crucifix. She knelt upon the metalled road itself, for what grief, what penance, what atonement, what solace, or in what ecstasy I could not begin to guess, but for all the world to see, beneath the wild sky. The effigy, I remembered, had on my first visit been of discreet plain stone, but now they'd fleshed it with gaudy cream paint, crowned it with brown hair and thorns and wounded it with pillar-box red. We sped on downhill without remark upon the penitent woman whoever she might be and whatever her prayerful purpose. McDonough could get a fire for £7 or £8, he said, and I would need mantles for the lamp. So he dealt, his mental cash-register whirring, as we rode, and I suppose I was easy game for a pig in a poke (the failing seems to be with me still), no matter how frugal I planned to be to last the year ahead upon my savings.

We halted in the old part of the village to let Maggie hop down. In the three years since my original visit the thatched dwelling with a red door, close beside the lane, that I'd remembered and assumed to be the one that I would rent, had been half razed. One room survived and this, as I'd discover, now served as a potato store. McDonough pointed out the cabin, tiled, and in a little plot, upon the other side of the lane, where I would stay and see my mock epic out. But now we came on through the puddles to the Feaneys' gate.

I was welcomed with some fuss, urged to sit in close to the range and given a cup of tea to fetch me round. A fry was begun but it bore so close a resemblance to my late lamented breakfast that I could hardly look it in the face.

'He'll not take his supper now,' said Mary brusquely.

'And why wouldn't he?' asked her mother, as she set the plate upon the table and urged me to eat for I must be starved. 'Now tell me,' she asked, a little to my disappointment, 'were you ever in Aran before?'

I told her I had eaten soda bread and jam and drunk cocoa at the very same table three years ago. But she couldn't remember, and even though I'd made some allusion to it when writing to enquire about a place to rent, it had not stayed in her mind. She had no recollection of any of it. Wasn't that a wonder? Mary sat sideways at the table, stiff and silent, fingering her cup, tweaking the handle between her nails, and now and then raising it to take a small sip.

'Sonny is in Kilronan on account of the dole or he would remember,' the old lady assured me. I picked bravely at my bacon and eggs. 'He would remember, surely.'

Mary sucked impatiently upon what remained of her teeth.

'Mind,' said Mrs Feaney, now picking up on another thread, 'he only gets eighteen shillings on account of the superannuation but it is a little holiday for him, you understand.'

She laughed lightly and sat back.

'And then do you see,' she resumed suddenly, 'if ever they brought any work here, patching the roads or the like, he'd be in line for it … Not that they do, mind.'

Mary tutted. I continued meanwhile to struggle with a slice of fried soda bread. And Mrs Feaney reflected, 'Not that they do … And sure, if there was any work Sonny would be too busy to do it anyway. Poor Sonny, he's a great one for work.'

Mary, pressed beyond endurance, said something sideways and sharp in Irish. Her mother merely chided her.

'Are you sorry for the cow or sorry for yourself, Mary Feaney? It is his only holidays to get the dole.'

Mary, whose holidays were never so well defined, sat a moment seething, then left the table sharply for the scullery to find the milk-can. The front door shuddered, the back door slammed, and she was gone.

'Ach, never mind Mary,' said her mother laughing, 'she's just cranky.'

My meal done, I was urged back to the warmth of the range. I sat and hoped my stomach would not rebel. The stove creaked and hummed like an old woman in stays busy at the hearth. Potatoes steamed in the pot, and steam, which also flew in wisps from the shins of my trousers, sealed the window, filtering what little daylight there was into the room. They would sit in the twilight and not light the mantle until nightfall. Salt now began to crystallize on my boots and trousers. The clock ticked beside the china cockerel. I half dozed. The cockerel stared beadily at the virgin with the dagger in her breast. She hung in a lugubrious frame upon the facing wall. Over the parlour lintel, over all, presided the trinity of pope, Christ and Kennedy. I began now to come back to my senses and to warm to the fact that I had at last arrived safe and sound at Kil-na-cer. Mrs Feaney took a taper and lit the gas in the globe; the light, beginning to sing like a little yellow canary, extinguished the last remains of the day.

The clock ticked. It was just gone five, apparently, nearer to six by my watch, which had got condensation in it and was difficult to read. But time in the wilderness is not dictated by clocks and watches. The clock is no wage slave's tyrant, no deadly dictator of deadlines, and no time-server. The clock is a toy, an inadequate façade before eternity, and like the emperor is unaware that it isn't wearing any clothes. Time on the island is measured by light and tide, the phases of the moon, weather and season. Although the clock may put a finger on the hour of daybreak or nightfall, its hands usher no one to work and call no one home. You may use it to meet or catch the boat by, in a most approximate fashion, or to be in time for school or Mass, but for much the greater part of its time a clock in an island kitchen is just an ornament with a small noise to it, a familiar spirit like the wind in the chimney or the gas in the globe. You would hear it most if it stopped. One thing the clock could never tell was closing time, and so it could not even suggest when Gregory might appear.

At first I thought it was the wind flurrying against the door, but this time the door flew open, announcing, with a perfectly timed pause, as if for a roll of drums, the prodigal's return. It was only eight, or was it nine o'clock, a modest holiday indeed, and Gregory came quietly, nothing obviously drunk or disorderly about him. Upright he seemed as the day I first beheld him. Suspiciously upright, on second thoughts, I guessed, as I rose to greet him and he strode in, forgetting the open door and the cold remnants of the storm behind him. He hung up his cap and oiler and then, slowly sensing something was amiss, turned back and gave the door a kick which, failing to connect, almost tipped him flat on the kitchen floor. By the time he had collected himself, Mary, who had been tutting about him for some time now, rose swiftly, pushed the door to, and swept off to bed.

However pleasantly befuddled he might be, Gregory was not confused as to who I was, although he wasn't sure he quite remembered my face.

'But then,' he said, settling into the chair opposite, fumbling to unlace his boots and putting on his sandles, 'but then?'

Unable to recall in the meantime what he had intended and having heard my story, he launched out upon a cautionary tale concerning the perils of Rossaveal and the dire nature of its inhabitants – the worst savages he knew in the whole world. There had been an occasion when he and his brother had crossed there to carry home a coffin, 'With a body in it, you understand,' he was especially amused to underline.

'Whose body was it now?' he paused to ask his mother, who was already once more busy at the frying pan.

'Only your own cousin, God save you and hold your talk.'

But God, thank God, could do nothing to silence Gregory that night (though he did a fair job of it through the rest of the week).

'We did cross early on a winter's morning. Out in February it was, the coldest day in the world, I'm telling you, and soon as we landed we went up the village to the pub for a drink, like, and do you know what I'm going to tell you?'

Mrs Feaney said something in Irish and Gregory rose and gained the table safely. She set his supper down before him and he began to eat.

'The buggers turned us away …'

He chewed and, emphasizing each word between bites, exclaimed, 'The … buggers … turned … us … away!' He waved a piece of ham on his fork. 'That would never happen on Aran. There are no locked doors on Aran, public house or no public house. But that's the kind of welcome you will find in Rossaveal … and a death in the family too. Would you ever believe what I'm telling you?'

I repeated that I'd not realized there was a village there, still less a pub, and explained again just how I'd waited, trusting that the boat would come.

'You had great good luck with the boat,' he said, coming back to his chair, 'great luck entirely … great luck,' and in that instant fell asleep.

While Gregory snoozed like an infant I decided I'd go out to take the air. I felt recovered, if a little sore in the midriff. Although the storm had all but died with the onset of night, you could feel a huge turbulence even in the deep lane, a commotion in the air that was the sea unwinding. Now and then the moon left a marble pattern or showed a chalky thumbnail as it raced the cloud. The clustered lights of the villages shone and flickered cosily: at nearby Kilmurvey, where a generator puttered to keep the post-office guesthouse blazing in luxury like an ocean-going liner; at half-hidden Gort na gCapall and at Oatquarter, both powered by gas and candlelight. I jumped the wall to the cabin McDonough had identified as mine and tried the door. I stumbled about the three dark rooms. I groped halfway up the rickety and hollow stair. But without a match to strike I could not see sufficiently to know what it was really like. So I retreated and walked on beyond the village to Kilmurvey, and on again to the bay where, in the storm's aftermath, huge swathes of seaweed rolled and churned, shadowy in the phosphorescent mouth of the sea. The reek of the sea might have knocked you over and at the same time prevented you from falling, so thick was it upon the air. The breakers pounded and unzipped with a hiss right down the length of the bay.

It must have been a combination of having been seasick and the salty ham I'd just been served but I began to feel thirsty. And since my mood was now quite euphoric and the night was young enough, I thought I'd mark the occasion with a little celebration and walked the hill to Dirrane's pub. In those days Dirrane's was a plain bar, a very sober setting, in a stone building beside a house in a little field just off the road. I pushed the heavy door open upon a pool of gaslight and silence. As I stood to order, the bald man at the bar did not lift his eyes from the Guinness as he moulded it into its glass, slicing and slicing the head off with a knife, with solemn attention, until it settled into a column of black with a wafer-thin head, no more than he had seemed to look up as I came in.

I glanced around. There were bare wooden benches against the walls and three or four tables. At one a group of men played cards. Others just sat before their drinks and stared. Here was the other edge to the word 'dole'. Apart from the hissing gaslight, the only sound was that of cards being knocked square after shuffling and the flicking of cards as they were dealt, the sweep of a hand and the rattle and chink of coins being drawn into a hoard, a glass being set back on a table, and the beat of your heart, perhaps, but not a word for minutes on end. A couple of old men made room for me to sit beside them. There were looks in my direction, there were smiles, but there was no talk, and nothing like the promise or expectation of it. The barman leant back, arms folded, chin on chest, and stared ahead at the door. It was the most solemn proceeding I had ever witnessed upon licensed premises, but it was nothing out of the usual. No one had died. The place was not in mourning. Dirrane's was just a dour pub. Some said it was the length of time he took to fill a glass that kept the customers so sober. But still there were 'incidents' at Dirrane's, and some men were barred, which was a hard fate because Dirrane's was the only bar outside Kilronan.

My first glimpse of a Dirranean 'incident' occurred that night.

I was just beginning to feel the benefit of my pint. A surcharge of well-being and excitement induced a state of reverie as, like my fellow drinkers, I stared ahead or paused to drink. I relived the crossing, without its discomfort. I stared happily at tomorrow and whatever it might bring. I planned and schemed and sank into myself. But I was soon enough roused when a man waving a bottle burst in and staggered up and down before the bar calling for drink. He was a slight man, with reddish straw-coloured hair, wearing a torn jacket of cheap blue cloth, his shirt half open down his chest, a typical Saturday-night figure you might meet with in any backstreet, in any ragged town, but hardly your prototypical man of Aran. His sudden entry caused little or no more stir among Dirrane's clientele than had my own. Dirrane himself stared past him as he stared past all the world. The man called for whiskey, though the bottle in his hand was still a quarter full. Dirrane served him. The man managed after some fumbling to spill neither money nor drink, to pay up, drink up and call for more. Once again he was served. Between refills he staggered up and down, to and fro, upon a stormy sea, and talked his head off about some incomprehensible grievance, some wrong or other, some misery. No one did anything to help him or restrain him. Dirrane took his money whenever he called for more and the men soberly raised their glasses to safety if he threatened to pitch against their table, and set them down again with remarkable gravity.

Eventually the game of cards was suspended. Frustrated and losing patience, the players began to urge Dirrane not to serve the poor man any more. But like one who had taken the licensed victuallers' Hippocratic oath and could not deny succour to a soul, Dirrane paid his complaining clientele no heed. The drunk had ceased to rail now and spoke only to demand more drink. He staggered up and down just as before but was watched more carefully, as a frisky bullock might be regarded down on the quay, as likely to cause an upset. With each drink he lurched back from the bar. It was all the same to him if he had something to lean against or not. He didn't know whether he was coming or going. He had just tipped a whiskey down his chin and, like a clown groping to catch an imaginary ball against the glare of an invisible sun, he moved this way and that, the glass upended on his mouth, still looking for the ball long after by any law of gravity it must have fallen. By now all eyes were on him and the atmosphere had turned a little sour. But the big elderly man next to the door had his eyes not so much upon him as upon his trajectory, gauging the amount of pitch and roll to his progress, and very smartly, at the perfect moment, he nipped to his feet with surprising agility, and opened the door so that the man fell out. He closed it upon him just as deftly and brushed the palms of his hands together, this way and that, as he sat down.

'Man overboard!' said my neighbour on one side, and said the other, in what was to me a mysterious allusion, 'That will teach him to twist rope.'

I slipped overboard myself a little later and never heard the drunk upon my way, missing presumed drowned in the black of night, the lost diaspora of dole day, and went aswim with Guinness to my bed, somewhere at sea between Shannon and Bloody Foreland.

3

## The Missus and the Modern Man of Aran

The morning dawned so still it stopped you at the door, as if
there were a sheet of glass between you and the day. Many mornings, with distant accompaniment of breaking waves, began in
such a fashion, in the pure sea-light of winter, but most unreally
after storms such as the one I had arrived in. Stand still and you
might wait an hour to hear a sound of human life. Sometimes
you'd wait a morning, the village growing eerie in its emptiness,
every dwelling a foundered *Marie Celeste*. Then you would know
it was probably a Sunday and you'd slept late. The rocks glistened
with wet, tarnishing only as the day grew and the rainfall drained
away. Among the lichen growths of grey and yellow and furry
brown patches of moss, above the waltzing sea, salt crystals grew
by afternoon. Like faint hints of quartz within the stone they left
irregular snail trails. Right through the year (even at times in the
bitter months of February and March), for several days on end,
the erratic climate could be hothouse warm, or, as they call it,

soft, bringing on ferns, or gentians, or primroses such as I found high among the sheltering rocks in December and January.

The island was too porous to be damp and in summer there were often droughts. Gregory carried precious spring water to his stock as if he were a Cretan. He had a homemade barrel, like a barrel cut in half, sealed at either end but with a large bung in the top, and a rope sling by which he bore it on his back the last stages from his cart, through narrow ways to corner fields. The previous summer had been unusually dry, resulting in a poor potato crop, which even as late as November men were now attending to, making clamps with bundles of rusty bracken and sand. But in the wintry ruins of Kil-na-cer, with a leak under the door and another near the ceiling, dampness is all. It must be driven out. And that is what I set about on my first morning. I drove not with a pitchfork but a shovel, stoking my grate as if it fed a steamship. I propped my mattress against two chair backs and stood it before the blaze. I boiled saucepans of water in the grate and scoured a selection of crockery from the dresser. Most of it had begun to crumble, its glaze being cracked and worn, and was unusable, but I found a tall milk jug and a mug and three or four plates, cobwebbed relics of some long-gone January sale in Galway. I unpacked my trunk and stored my things away. As the ashes spilt and gathered in the hearth I carried buckets of coal from the pigsty that now doubled as a coal-hole and lavatory and sent up new smoke signals in declaration of my occupation. The fire drew straight up to the sky. On cold days starlings would line up around my chimney and burble and bicker there like guttersnipes. On wet days the rain would hiss in the coals, and if it hailed, as once in a while it did, the hailstones bounced straight into the room. What heat there was that didn't go to heaven, rose to the roof and up into the loft. Soon I would devise ways of preserving my coals and make my fire serve me rather than its own gods, wherever they resided, now in a flock of starlings, now in a bowl of stars.

So I began in ignorance to discover the pattern of my life ahead, to learn about time as space, whether night or day, and forget it as linear tyranny. I became absorbed in domesticities. Not only was my husbandry a satisfaction in itself, in good times seamless with my days and nights, it also helped eke out my balance at the Bank of Ireland. There a too-familiar, inexorable time still ticked away in fatal columns of credit and debit, like a bomb on a long fuse.

Discounting the little lean-to against my back door, constructed by Gregory with the aid of a government grant and housing a sink and a tap, my house had five small rooms: three on the ground floor and two lofts. The loft to the south-east, behind the chimney-breast and above my bedroom, lit by a draughty gable window, was reached by a crooked wooden stair that ran up the back wall of the kitchen. It contained on its bare boards an iron bedstead with a horsehair mattress. The other, north-westerly loft – once a turf loft – was boarded off and blind dark. The boards, and the door set in them, accessible only by ladder, formed a bulkhead against the draughts, and contributed much to the timbered magnificence of my ark-like, upturned boat of a kitchen. The kitchen ceiling itself rose to the roof's apex timbered with narrow tongue-and-groove planking. Stained and additionally darkened with soot, the boards ran from the height of the walls (perhaps seven foot) in a perfect sweep to meet in an arch about the roof-high, whitewashed chimney-breast at one end and against the planked bulkhead on the other. In workmanship this cavernous enclosure – otherwise a poky affair with a bare stone floor, a dresser, a table, two wooden and two old lounging fireside chairs – was as uncharacteristically professional as the lavish use of timber was untypical. So much timber seemed unreal on Aran where scarcity of wood is so marked, the island being almost totally treeless, with only a few stunted hazels and sallies in hospitable hollows.* The limestone-loving fuchsia might burgeon on a village wall or an ornamental evergreen throw a rare wind-bent shadow in a garden or against a house-side (but I can remember only one outside Kilronan). Blackthorn on the rocks grew surreptitiously, serpentine, flattened out by the wind in long arms or bent queerly around boulders.

Foraging for timber became a main task of my days. If I found none on the shore I could always climb to the Dún and reach in among the ragged fringe of rocks for the thorn branches that subsisted there. I was always on the lookout for wood. I developed a nose for even the least resinous sea-dried spar buried in the tidemark's tangled seaweed or jammed between the seaward rocks. I came to regard the merest fish-box splinter with exaggerated enthusiasm, as a superstitious believer might a piece of the true cross in Rome. Nor was I alone. Along the shore there was often to be found a bevelled plank or spar, or a hoard of miscellaneous pieces great and small, stacked together, like a quaint shrine, an altar to some obscure deity, and topped by a stone with which its finder

---

*The Second World War was a boon time for timber, washed up from torpedoed convoys. Gregory showed me the salvaged beams, great hulks of timber, that had been used to build various of his outhouses.

marked his claim. Such claims would stand for months respected, indeed might, I supposed, stand for ever, if their claimants died having never found time to bear them home. Gregory would instance the practice as an illustration of the islanders' scrupulous respect for each other's property and labour. (A cynic might add that the chances of getting caught at even so disguisable an offence as stealing driftwood, of being seen and of being known, were too high to contemplate. There were always invisible eyes on the island to see who came and went and when and where, a case of closely observed lanes.)

I hoarded my timber with my coals and in a tea-chest in the alcove by my fire. When too sea-cured it burnt like tinder but always with a peacock-tail eye of vivid flame. More resinous spars and logs, though hard with my blunt saw to reduce to grate-sized pieces, might burn like fireworks at first, with a fizz and a crack, but they burnt well and made my eventual ton of coal (£14) last through the year with more coal to spare at the end of my stay than I'd inherited on my arrival. There being no true surface soil to the island, let alone bogland, peat had to vie with coal and coal was the more economical fuel, if infinitely less pleasing to the nose. Sometimes I found a turf or two washed ashore but I had to strain to believe that it burnt at all well once soused. The days when it came by hooker to Kilmurvey were gone and peat now belonged with the picturesque, though I sometimes caught a whiff of it on my increasingly rare visits down the island to Kilronan.

That first day slipped away to sea almost like a dream, and evening found me taking supper at the Feaneys' table. Our agreement was simple. For £12 a month I had my house, all the potatoes I could eat, and all the carrots and turnips I might want from the garden abutting my own and old Maggie Faherty's cabin, which stood upon its other side. For 6d a day I filled my jug with milk, and when there was soda bread to spare, a loaf or half a loaf was put aside for me. Old Mrs Feaney had insisted that I take my meals that day with them. So we sat round the table to eat our salt ham, potatoes and vinegary beetroot, and when we had done and Mary had cleared away, her lot being to skivvy, we drew up to the stove. Pacified by his labour, Gregory reclined to one side of me, and Mrs Feaney sat to the other. Mary eventually, in her choric role, settled behind us, at the table, with an impatient sideways air, as if she might depart at any moment.

'Well, and how are you liking Aran?' the old lady began, as she would often begin, and I made an account of my day. (Her other habitual enquiry was 'Any news?' News being even rarer on Aran than wood, the merest splinter of information might serve to excite the mind and make time run. I must myself have been a bonus.) Gregory had been out on the rocks from dawn rebuilding a wall levelled by the storm. There was some talk of walls and the labour they entailed and what pitiful nothing they enclosed. They marked out property, whether acres of stone without covering, or cultivable loam, and mapped its troubled history. The land wars had been bitter on the island and left an ineradicable trace in memories much given to grievance. Gregory, being an economist of the old school, believed in 'land'. It may not have been the way of the future but it was an article of faith with him. He framed his life upon what he knew and scorned those from whom he bought – a crooked field of rocks here, a garden there – to increase his store, which also grew by inheritance as family lines died out. He believed in land and he believed in hard work. Let those who would idle on the dole, with a grant for this and a grant for that and scarce a hand's turn to help themselves, do so if it pleased them.

The talk of walls caused Mrs Feaney to recall one that ended abruptly in the middle of the rocks (her children knew its location all too well, not far before the ball alley, this side of Kilmurvey).

'Because Paddy did lift a stone there once and heard a voice speak from under it, would you believe?' she appealed to me, peering over her glasses, 'and he set it back where he found it and never went back there and there the wall is standing to this day.' She laid her hands in her lap, and paused for emphasis, 'And the stone itself —'

But Gregory had grown restless until his impatient nature got the better of him.

'Sure that's all imagination,' he butted in abruptly, 'just imagination.'

You could see it was a routine they'd been through more than once before. But the old woman had seized her chance and stubbornly had her fling at the story once again. If she could, she would have drawn me in upon her side. Had I known the humour of the family better I might have let her, to encourage more talk, for which prize almost any position might justifiably be sacrificed. But Gregory wanted nothing to do with it and, having laid the ghostly voice, smiling at me in a confiding way, he now propped his sandalled feet upon the fender and asked to be excused should he doze off.

'Poor man,' his mother granted, unruffled by their skirmish, 'he's working all hours, late and early. He has no holidays like yourself, sir.'

I smiled to show, as I hoped, that I understood. But Gregory spoke what appeared to be a mild reproach, and Mary threw in her few Irish pence. They all regularly discussed what I took to be minor niceties regarding me from their Irish vantage in this way. Later, when we knew each other better, they would hold the same court in English, sometimes switching between the one language and the other. This time their mother, smiling benignly at me, dismissed them with just a couple of words and looked back down at her work. She was crocheting something from a ball of coarse cream wool. Not, it seemed, as tired as he thought, Gregory now pulled a copy of the *National Geographic* magazine from the side of his chair. In a moment, without preamble, he began to read aloud an article on the Indian tribes of Latin America. He read steadily, in a monotone, stumbling only, as anyone might, over foreign words and names like 'Guarani-Tupi', and we all listened, until, touching upon the annual rainfall in the Amazon basin, he provoked Mary to remark with a snort of mock contempt that it was wetter on Aran, anyway.

'But it did not rain today,' I said.

'It was a great day,' said Gregory, well-being personified, setting down his magazine and yawning, 'a great day entirely.'

'T'will rain tomorrow, I'd say, anyway,' scoffed Mary and sat with her mouth briefly but characteristically ajar, halted by a sudden self-consciousness that sent a flush through the pallor of her cheek. We sank into silence, as if allowing each other pause for reflection. In the end, less comfortable as a guest to sit and say nothing for my supper, I asked Mrs Feaney what she was making.

'Ah, nothing,' she said, 'nothing. 'Tis only a bonnet for Sonny. I have the wool over from a sweater and it will be handy for him out in the month of February. We get no winter in Aran until the month of February, isn't it funny? When the wind is not up it is very soft altogether. It is rainy too,' she threw in, nodding at Mary, 'but the rain is healthy.'

Gregory was now snoring, his toothless mouth a little 'O' between the upward jut of his chin and the downward hook of his nose. (Combined with his ruddy complexion, his features always put me in mind of the face on an old cock salmon.) Mary soon departed.

'That girl is fearful cranky,' said Mrs Feaney and continued her crochet.

I made to go but then, looking up, she said, 'And you will be missing the missus now?'

Had she been waiting her moment? If a man has a wife no mention of her should take him by surprise, unless he has a bad conscience. The problem was I was not married. In a flash of naïvely tactful idiocy I had written, while making arrangements about the house, to say my wife might join me in the summer. I didn't want to offend anyone by going against the local mores, so I ended up testing them by lying. In the meantime my girlfriend had landed a job she wished to keep and, though I held out hope, in the end it gave her wiser, second thoughts about taking a holiday. Things cooled. No further shuffling coils of explanation will I give you. But be advised, if you must sow a lie, make it a decent one. Boast, for example, that you killed your father. The impulse to patricide is forgivable in anyone. As a metaphor it knows no equal in the Freudian calendar or in the Roman. Steer clear of marriages.

If the lying hurt me, that was no more than I should have expected. (I'd rather suppress it here as trivial absurdity but it has too nice a denouement for that.) I'd explain nothing. I'd not dwell on it. I'd ride the emotional weather out in the lee of my larger adventure. My error remained with myself. It is an iniquity to be punished by the judges, I told myself. So I stepped out into the starless night, and made my blind way home, feeling, as I shortly told my journal, that this moment marked the true beginning of my stay.

Indoors I struck a match and lit a candle. The darkness seemed to thicken about me and then to thin and to shadow. I lit another, stirred the embers, threw some driftwood on the fire; in a sudden instant, flame lit up the room, almost to its height, and seemed to concentrate everything. That night too I began a ritual I would keep of making my porridge for the morning. I had two saucepans, one fitting the other like a sleeve, and so could steam a perfect porridge of the thickest oats I'd been able to buy. While the porridge bubbled and puttered and the saucepans steamed and rattled I also began by the light of my Calor gas globe to write my journal, noting things I'd heard people say and things I'd seen and done. I scribbled that night, for example, of a visit to Kilmurvey strand:

*In the wake of the storm I collected an armful of driftwood. The sea was still wound up and lunging after being driven so hard. The silver crescent of the bay lay enveloped in its booming. Waders scarcely audible shrilled and flew and realighted at its mouth. Its mouth was full of churning seaweed. On my way back I saw a man zig-zagging slowly on his bike behind three red calves and two red cows, along the old road* beneath the dune. (*This I later realized was Gregory's brother Bart-ley.*) *Two women came the opposite way, from Kilmurvey, coated, head-scarved. One climbed right down onto the sand to pass the cattle safely. At the far end, where the road comes down from Kilmurvey, a tall youth emerged from the dune with curragh oars over his shoulder and lugging a box. He crossed the strand and set his burden down just out of reach of the waves. I went up and spoke to him. He was deeply self-conscious but explained that he was going out to get some lobsters from a store cage in the bay, the catch of the past month, the last of the season. They were going over to Connemara on the boat that evening. They'd get 15/– a pound for them. Some would weigh 2-3lb. Another, shorter, older man in a peaked cap arrived. He greeted me in a cursory way as if to let me know he was busy. They got under one of the bee-tle-backed curraghs that lay above the strand and set off, making it look easier than it must be to carry such a vessel off the ledge and down through the soft sand to the water. They put their box aboard and, the young man rowing already, the older one skipped deftly in and began to pull upon his oars. The curragh reared up once, twice and three times before they skimmed away. (One meaning I've read somewhere for the word 'curragh' is 'unstable'.) When they returned – with 38 lob-sters (suppose they averaged 2lb = 76x15 = 760+380 = 1140/– = £57, at a minimum = £14.5.0 a week) – I carried the oars back up the strand for them. (The oars have no blades to speak of and are square for much of their length, scarcely even bevelled, with a hole for the thole pin, through a triangular wooden flange. They call them sticks.) The youth delayed me and gave me three crab claws, 'to be putting in the fire, like'. His boss railed at him, over some detail regarding the storing of the lobsters. 'Don't be making a haims of it, now,' he said twice over. What is 'a haims', however you spell it? The sky kept clear. The Twelve*

*Pins in Connemara looked unreal on the horizon. I took my wood home to tend my fire before it might go out. Outside the corner house, an incident. Two young men were bending over a mo-ped, from which they'd removed the chain wheel, one helping the other whose machine it was. (A young girl with brilliant red hair played on the doorstep, stepping up and down, on and off the bottom step, her back straight, her hands stiffly at her side as if dancing a jig.) I greeted them and stopped to pass the time of day. But the black-haired one most engaged in the problem was gruff. I stayed a while, leaning on the wall in what I thought was a friendly, hail fellow way. But in a moment the black-haired one came round the wall and, squaring up to me, demanded a fight. He nodded in the direction of a nearby field and said we should go there. For some odd reason I found myself looking out of the corner of my eye at the little field, as if involuntarily sizing it up, instead of exclusively sizing him up. I shrugged at him and said I saw no reason why we should go to such trouble. I was in no doubt that he meant business, until he turned away and went muttering back to his work. I saw his companion smirk. The girl kept playing on the step, and I went on my way, saying (absurdly) goodbye.*

That was Colm and we were almost coevals, he being perhaps a couple of years older than me. Colm resented me and always spoiled to fight me. We would have our day, in the end, and make an uneasy peace, a sort of friendship. He lived literally between a rock and a hard place, a recipient of doles, part-sharer in a small fishing boat without means to make it seaworthy, with nothing you could call a creature comfort, not a thread of carpet but cold floors, and draughty windows, no wife for company, no hope of one upon the horizon, a father in the mental hospital at Ballinasloe, a mother ostracized for the love-child she'd had by a visiting labourer, who rarely stepped out of doors, whom I never saw until one evening in the spring. 'Somebody has to stay, boots or no boots,' Colm would say when talk of another's opportunity arose. 'We can't all be leaving.' To him I was a fool and my presence an idle affront. And could you begin to question his position? But I am surprised now to think how little perturbed I was by his hostility. The Connacht fashion is or was to come to blows, for your enemy or enemies to waylay you on a black night and give you a clattering, a kind of folk justice that led to vendettas, such as the one much later in my story I discovered Gregory to be embroiled in and in which I played a minor part. There were subplots and intrigues in the island that a stranger might never discover, whose roots found nourishment where nothing else might flourish. But I came on to be shaken from a pensive mood, induced by Colm's welcome, because I met again with old Michael Gill. Hailing me as he rode towards me, perched sideways on his mare's rump, off to gather seaweed, with two panniers on a straddle, he called, 'All Dublin knows you're in it, mister.' He often hauled in Dublin in this style. Its metropolitan incongruity seemed to amuse him and to point to the vanity of life. When in the better weather he came by and saw me at the high gable, reaching from my ladder, having whitewashed the front of the house and now working round, he gibed, 'You have done the Dublin end, anyway.' On another sortie that first day, this time to spy out a suitable fishing ground for setting a line over night, I re-encountered Michael:

*The shore being littered with fresh wrack or ribbon weed, Michael had come down to load some for his garden. His real interest was in the long claw-footed stalks. He gathered these into bundles and forked the bright, translucent ribbons into the panniers, his mare standing steadily as the load mounted. Once he had filled one pannier, he led her round and filled the other. Then he forked a load across her back, art-fully, for almost none slipped off and it was as slippery as eels, until the horse looked like a dromedary. The hump was secured with cords, from corner to corner, as it were. Before he led the mare back up the strand, he stooped and gathered armfuls of the long, rubbery weed stems and carried them up to the ledge and laid them there. 'Sea-candles' he called them, and seeing what he was doing I helped him. This was idyllic Aran, the sea pounding, the waders whistling, the air as clear as air can be. I'm not sure he appreciated my uninvited assistance but he bore it with patience and explained the seaweed business. How he would set the sea candles to dry through the year and sell them to the agent, for £13 a ton. 'But if another man did work here, I would not. There would not be enough in it for two men, you understand? That's how it is.' Normally he worked along the shore, a little to the west, he said. He pointed it out to me, round beyond the cottages. I asked what the agent did with it. 'They do send it to Holland for making ladies' stock-ings. That kind of way.' 'Holland?' I asked him, for some reason thinking it odd. 'Holland amn't I telling you,' and picking up a bun-dle he exclaimed, a little testily, 'and how it is I cannot tell you ...' In the old days they used to burn the kelp for iodine. The mare struggled up onto the road, the seaweed hump rocking wildly as she made the last step up off the sand. I went on to find some winkles on the rocks, pick-ing them out from among the bladderwrack, and prised off limpets with my knife. I thought I'd lay a line across a delta of shingle and sand between some rocks and see if the tide would bring me luck. But really the tide wasn't right and I held off. I'll need to wait, for low tide to turn in late evening.*

*

You soon find in a new home, especially when it is an old one, and above all at night, a gamut of noises, inside and out, that habit and familiarity will silence. They are the ground bass of solitude, and the grace notes. In the blare of modern life who hears them through the cacophony and cotton-wool? Only the unfortunate, the misfits, and the mad, or whoever might be disturbed by love or grief. As I sat scribbling, absorbed in my efforts, my porridge cooling on a ledge in the hearth, the coals subsiding, I became aware of a perpetual, almost inaudible tinkling noise at my door. Although so very quiet, its persistence, once I noticed it, made it sound loud. In the end I had to go to see what it was and, closing the first pages of my journal for the night, rose to inspect my door. Of course the moment I opened it the noise disappeared. So I shut myself out with it and bent my ear. Some part of the doorknob, a ring, a thin loop of brass, had worked loose and in the slightest breeze it tinkled like a cymbal. This little noise, drowned only by boisterous weather and only still on breathless days, kept me company through the year.

I went back in. You can imagine how it felt to close my door for, as I thought, the last time that night, to stir the embers, to extinguish the gas globe, to carry a wobbling and shadowy candle flame across the room, and so to bed. The door seemed oddly light and insubstantial against the press of the night, a not quite still and never a silent night, which sounded as I'd stood upon the threshold, staring out, taking the ocean air, like a giant conch shell at my ear. And so I went to bed, but as I sank through the sea of unfamiliar sounds I kept resurfacing. Nor was it simply the

mice that disturbed me, though they rattled overhead and tin-
kered in the kitchen and sent their advance guard across the
linoleum to inspect the tundish on the chair beside my bed, to
explore the central massif of my couchant form, to gnaw, as I dis-
covered next day, the end off my fountain pen. What bliss it must
have been in the days of that other visitor from Wales, Giraldus
Cambrensis, who found the island mouse-free.* Was it the same
island? But mice or no mice, tinkling cymbals or no tinkling cymbals, I couldn't sleep. My mind raced and I didn't feel tired. So I
rose and dressed, put on my boots and oilskin, stuffed into my
poacher's pocket three rashers in a piece of newspaper, a little
folding pan to fry them in, a corner of soda bread, some kindling,
some cheese, some biscuits, and went out. Did I say scarcity of
wood? The island night resembled nothing better than a tall
wood hushing and soughing in the winter air. As I stole and
stumbled my way down onto the metalled road by the corner
house at Kilmurvey, the augmented roar of the sea rose up to
meet me and with it the pungent smell of seaweed. I could see
nothing, not a star, but knew the cloud was low from feeling it
damp upon my face and hands.

As I had done the previous night, but now at a much later
hour, I found my way down beside the graveyard on its promontory and onto the road beneath the dune, and there I loitered a
while listening to the sea and watching for the flash of breakers
which like a silvery lighthouse beam penetrated the murk as the
waves swept along the shore. I had it in my mind to walk the low

---

*Giraldus Cambrensis visited and wrote about Ireland and, it seems, Aran, in
1184. Translators debate whether he meant mice or rats. In Irish rats are called
'French mice'. Either way, rats or mice, they were both abundant on Inishmore.

road to the east, perhaps to see the dawn from Dog's Head, near Straw Island where the lighthouse stood, beyond Killeany, and turned that way at last; but as I turned, a voice, a cough (a sheep perhaps?), nearly jumped me out of my skin, filled me with a momentary terror. Then at my back in a gap in the retaining wall a figure slid down. 'God to you,' he said to me in Irish, an unearthly notion at an unearthly time of night, to which I was lost for speech to return him the correct response, 'God and Mary to you'. It was doubly dark under the wall but light enough to tell a man's bulk (not great), and you don't need eyes to know if he is sober. He asked me for a light (in Irish he would ask for 'a reddener', something to redden the end of the cigarette, as readers of James Joyce will know) and although I didn't smoke I had my matches, to make a fire, or to ease my way to a candle should it still be dark when I went in. I struck a match for him and attempted to cup it but it blew out at once, making everything darker in its brief aftermath. I fumbled and struck another and held it while the man, cupping his own hands half about mine, nursed the flame to his half stub of a Sweet Afton. I saw not enough to know him by but a glimpse of the cigarette pack in his horny hand.

Though we walked half the island together in the dark, talking sporadically, mostly about how and why I had come to be on Aran, on which he passed no comment, I could never know him again, by sight at least. He would have been able to pick me out as the stranger beyond at Kil-na-cer, but if he ever saw me on the road he chose not to show it. By chance I did in the end identify him, one wild night in Kilronan, in the summer months, in Conneely's American Bar. I recognized his drunken, semi-coherent story, with its memorable refrain: 'Three days and nights … three days and nights … with a dead man in a curragh before we were washed up on the shores of County Clare.'

It was a classic story. They'd been fishing when the seas uprose. A man went overboard and was swept away. By a miracle they came (but too late) upon his body. They heaved him aboard, but were now an oarsman short, and a drowned corpse the heavier, and the sea took them, but could not capsize them. I had spoken, inevitably, of my crossing, it still looming large in my tender mind, and said I hoped one day nonetheless to find someone to take me out in a curragh. It launched him on his tale of what the sea had done to him, and how I should be wise and keep my feet upon the land and not be tempting fate. Even the dry land had its sea-perils. 'I think I know every … or a lot of things and every drowning that ever happened in this island,' he advised me, and he spoke of an incident when fifteen men had drowned, in the year of 1852 on the flagstones by Killeany. It was an incident of which I would often hear tell. The only drowning of which I heard in my time was of a youth on Inishmaan, swept from a rock while fishing. By the time my companion came to part from me, down some obscure passage on the outskirts of Kilronan, he had entered into the jocular island-of-doom mode. 'Ah, but it does be a Mickey Mouse country now, altogether, and no mistake, all Mickey Mouse, amn't I telling you? Mickey Mouse and Donald Duck. They do be the men of Aran for you now.'

The watches of the night are long and made to sap your wildest waking dreams. By three or surely by four in the morning who would not regret being still upon the road, who set out from home at half past midnight to find the morning? When is the dawn?

When will the thinning day begin? I walked until I ran out of road and, stumbling hopelessly upon the dunes, turned and walked the way I'd come, through the tucked-up shadows of Killeany and Kilronan, my new boots galling. With the night at last blowing fitfully clear and starry I found the old road and set out upon it, a road that seemed interminable but one with scarce an incline.

I heard the morning before I saw it, rattling with rain at my window, droning and clattering round the house, pushing the rude day in my face, reproaching me for a malingerer without use or purpose. Your own company can seem at times to be too much like the middle of the night for comfort, without a star in sight, and the rain coming on, cutting a swathe across the kitchen floor. So I roused myself to stir the grate and get my porridge warming, and went to my oilskin's copious inner pocket to retrieve the rashers of bacon, but mysteriously I failed to find them there, nor any kindling, nor cheese, nor bread of any kind, as if I'd dreamt about them. But then, as I puzzled and wondered if I wasn't going mad, or if I hadn't indeed risen from a peculiarly potent dream, I found them swinging in the bottom of the lining.

The rain fell, and would continue to fall all day and night and for three days more. It blew upon a gathering storm, and flattened the view against my window, so that the sea shooting high above the distant rocks looked as if it erupted from Bartley Feaney's garden.

## 4

## *Fish, Flesh and Folly*

In autumn and the early days of winter, geese were sometimes blown towards the island, or sought the lough to break a journey. I saw such a flock that day wind up in ragged bands far down below the road above Kilronan. Coming away from Oghil Lough, they rose and rose to blend in the grey and stormy heights of migrant cloud, and made a skein beyond Killeany. Wild geese are a sight as ancient as Ireland. Once seen in their element, they'll flash for ever upon the inward eye and echo in the inward ear, those sentries against time's tyranny and other oppressions great and small. They stopped me in my tracks, that drenching Atlantic morning, high on the island's shoulder. Wobbling, buckling, mending, blurring smokily in the blowing rain, something like ideas taking shape or memories themselves, they got under way and formed at last an arrowhead, fixed upon a greener elsewhere. Or so I fancied as I watched them out of sight. I later made a draft of these verses in my journal:

They so rarely reach here now
You'd be forgiven for thinking you're dreaming,
The dream of eternity, or some such,
You with your goose-wing westward prospect,
And a puddle blowing at your door:

Demisting your spectacles in a cloud of linen,
Squinting across the flapping morning
To see how their true aim's flown,
With an arrow-head as variable as any head,
Wavering in a smudged heaven.

We had lead grey in surfeit on Aran and goose grey too, but green was too thin on the ground to fatten geese, and what Lilliputian stubbles there were had been gleaned to the last grain, as if by fastidious mice. But if most of the wild geese had flown, some still lingered, as I was to learn when, next morning, I saw the island's lighthouse-keeper greet me at the peep of day. I was leaning in my doorway with a mug of tea, about to set off for the shore, in the dark new daylight, taking the dawn neat off the ocean air. He halted astride his bicycle, just in the lane before me, and held up a limp-necked greylag goose. I raised a hand and called to salute him. On he went, triumphant, the bird back in his basket, gun tied to crossbar, bearing manna from the wintry heavens. He would not see its like again all season. He would talk of nothing else that day, of how he stalked the little flock and yet could hardly see, and how he crept among the rocks and how he stood to shoot, as the geese rose, and hit one, dark though it was, by more luck than he would ever own to, or so I fancied.

Apart from the weekly sacrifice of mutton, imported from Galway for the purpose, by the butcher at Oatquarter, fresh meat, as opposed to salt-cured, smoked, or tinned varieties, rarely found its way to the winter menus of our village. The era of the Frigidaire and the deep freeze was yet to come in 1968. Nightfall at nearby Kilmurvey heard the putt-putt-puttering of the guest-house generator and of that at the big house too. But our neighbours there mostly dwelt, as we did, by candlelight, oil light, and gas globe. How many homes might have been illuminated for the cost of two generators? I do not know. I suppose an entire community such as ours. But though a community there was, skeletal yet interwoven, stressed with resistances and rivalries, and bound together by affections and loyalties, tragedy and comedy, common necessity no longer held it as intimately together as once it had. It was a symptom of the modern age, the incipient self-help era. And this was striking to observe because the past remained such an immediate neighbour. So intimate was it that some still wore its clothes next to their skin, and occupied its houses, and tuned their mindsets to its fading wavelength.

In Bartley Feaney's kitchen, at the edge of Kil-na-cer, there hung above the hearth a painting, the work of some visiting lady. It showed the village as it had been forty or fifty years before. A cluttered settlement, it stood along a narrow lane, set among high-walled gardens. My home, then bonneted with straw, on its little promontory of rock, figured there, showing its tall gable end and the corner of a window. You could stand in the ruined old village now (I have already described it for you) and try to imagine the spaces filled again with homes and stores and pigsties, with whitewash and thatch and bright red doors and blue doors, with poultry round them, and all human life going in and out, where now stood foundations of old cottages, roofless gables and walls. It was a world more remote and arduous, more neglected by the world outside, more populous and purposeful, than in my time. It worked together to survive, not quite as portrayed in Flaherty's famous film, but also in epic ways. (Most of Kil-na-cer's few residents were veterans of it.) Too many had now died or otherwise departed, too few had married, too few been born, too much had been erased and razed, too many patches overgrown for you to re-imagine what the artless painting gave you at a glance. The inch-meal past was of course still dispersing. You found it in Gregory's store, where he kept his cart and jaunting cars, the one with the metal-rimmed wheels, the de luxe model with rubber rims. There, with the cobwebbed redundant spinning wheel and loom, and bundled drift-nets slung beneath the roof, it lay in its half-way house, the dark air dry with the tang of rust and earth, and oblivion. You found it with a suitcase at the harbour. But it was still busy and fluent enough in the Irish language, or otherwise at the Feaneys' table, where the evening scene, and the fare itself, was closer to that in Van Gogh's 'The Potato Eaters' than to anything you are likely to know or remember.

None in our vicinity but the lighthouse keeper was a wild-fowler. But, without a gun, I supplemented my diet modestly with fish and occasionally a rabbit. My misspent boyhood and youth now proved well spent. Those half-delinquent years had taught me at least how to nightline for a fish, and how to net a rabbit through a drystone wall. That morning I was about to go to inspect a line I had set the previous evening. My efforts so far had been spoiled by the weather and twice my tackle had to be abandoned in a tangled mess of weed. But combing on the shore I found a small blue buoy, part of some fishing gear half buried in the sand, and it inspired me to a change of approach. Instead of fishing horizontally, stringing a line between pegs on the storm beach, I moved a quarter of a mile or so along the shore, north-west beyond the clochán, and with the aid of my prized blue buoy fished vertically, a few yards in from the previous night's low-tide mark, in the direction of Craghalmon, where the cormorant in satanic guise hung out his heraldic wings to dry. This was the shoreline that old Michael Gill worked, low and rocky, with every gradation of weed to find within the span of a spring tide, from bladderwrack to kelp, from black weed to red. When the sea was up and I met him down there, forking candles from the tidemark, it sometimes seemed he was a gardener in Eden. For so he called it, albeit in his mocking way, turning to survey it, straightening, like an expectant mother, the base of his back against the heel of his hand.

'It does be,' he paused to push his cap back off his brow, 'my sea-side holidays, my … Howth Head, my Phoenix Park … my land of milk and honey … my … Garden of Eden, my el-dor-ado.' He threw out an arm to encompass it in a sweeping gesture, then retracted his hand to scratch the side of his head, and paused to think, but thought remaining too long in its ashes, he turned away to pick some weed-stalks.

'My Boston tea party,' incongruously arose at last, 'my United States, my Yukon, my … Fort Knox.'

And so he went on, piling one thing on another, as was his manic style, adding a phrase almost for each candle he picked, as if to show you just what his back-breaking (heart-breaking) world was not, and what he knew of the world, until he stood again and added with apparent finality, 'my Bank of Ireland vaults'. Yet he was not quite done without his favourite refrain: 'But there is nothing for nothing, only the briars on the rocks and the seaweed on the strand. That's how it is, that kind of way.' He would quench his half-bitter humour in silence until I took my leave. He seemed to believe his life to be little more than a charade, for which working on the shore was a therapy. His wife and he had brought their sons up well. Two still lived beneath their roof, but the others were all of them Yanks, Dublin Yanks, English Yanks, and Yanks in New England where the species was invented. What more was there to do but draw his dole, soft-soap and plunder summer tourists, and wait to die? It preyed upon him more and more, even as I knew him, he and his penchant for the graveyard monologue. A final measure of his doom, if not his sense of doom, were the dried seaweed bundles, stacked on Kilmurvey harbour wall by the month of May. They were still there in the autumn when I bade Michael and his family good-bye. The agent never came for them and so I believe a tradition ended.

Even on grey and overcast days the light seemed to glare up from the mottled rocks and pebbles and to hang in the dried grasses on that shore. The surf cast its own light, and the sea-sound swelled overhead in a dome. Once you fell into the habit, you could forget time there completely. I would sometimes lie up there on soft days, where Michael could not see me (but, if I cared to, I could see him). Up beyond the corner of the last field, lounging like a playboy, I listened to the gulls and waders and the constant inconstant sea (I love you, I love you not) plucking at the shore. I would be waiting for the tide or not waiting for anything, not mulling over the meaning of life, nor pondering, certainly, the origins of our moral struggle. But drawing as near to matter as I might, to the stones and the weather, half dozing, half aware of Michael pottering, cloud drifting, light shifting, with gentle zephyrs and balmy breezes buzzing at my ears, I tried not to try to be at ease, and met with some success.

It felt like my métier – rare the happy times when we can think what we like and say what we like. How placid time is when you track it down to its source. Earth has process and season, birth and death, but time is a human invention, bred of the sale of labour and the price of leisure. So once – but perhaps no more? – childhood in its blissful ignorance knew, without reflection. Meanwhile, the absent cashier, as I fancied, shot a sidelong glance at the clock, wiped his thumb upon his tongue, and continued counting. On the island I heard it said, with satiric exaggeration, stereotyping the mythic Celt, that if it took one man a day to dig a field, it took two men two days. Exaggeration or stereotype or neither, it was the arithmetic of a god I could imagine serving.

Others worked that shoreline too, at low tide, according to obscure historic territories and rights, cutting weed or collecting winkles (no longer for the Billingsgate market but for the table or for bait). But the world was empty as I stepped out, the thin morning grey and blustery. The Sound ran in turmoil, ran like a river in spate. For the winds had mounted as night fell and the sea would take till evening to subside, unless yet again the weather turned around.

Watching the sea for a small blue buoy (at daybreak, facing eastwards) is like tuning a radio to a lost signal. In such a way you might search the world for meaning to hang the empty hat of your soul upon. Was that it, bobbed upon the chopping waves? Blue into grey will go, as any painter knows, and blue into green. An orange buoy is more seaworthy. But the first rule when nightlining is to rise before your gear shows, or the gulls will steal your breakfast, should breakfast be served. It is, besides, impossible to oversleep when you have a line out, or so I used to find. I would toss and roll all night, as if I was at sea, checking my watch at least once an hour, and so I had spent the previous night. My sleep pattern had anyway been irregular since my arrival and my mind inclined to race once I lay down.

A seasoned fisherman will prove no stranger to disappointment. His capacity to believe in his luck must guarantee it. He puts faith in his instinct, trust in his judgement, as to the lie of a piece of shoreline and the odds that the weather will hold. Yet even a hundred hooks in the ocean are as so many needles in a haystack two thirds the size of the world. When I was a youth I would sometimes risk a hundred hooks, but a haul of twelve fish, and one for luck, and I knew the seas were lavish. That was in the estuary upon ribbed sand. Now all that water is polluted, and even then it had begun to be. I had never set lines among and upon rocks before, rocks draped with weed at the dank low-tide mark, where the sea sucked and glugged in unseen caverns and holes, where footing was unsure and the currents beneath might draw you who knew where? There lurked the conger with the bark and the bite of a dog and what other monsters? Nor had I fished such pure wild seas before.

I made my tackle by first sewing an anchoring rock into a bag of netting. This was stout stuff, ideal for my purpose, from the sock end of a trawl I had found among some jetsam. After lowering the anchor on a rope until it stuck fast in a hole, I tied my heavy fishing line to the rope, with twelve baited hooks, and some old cork floats at the join, before casting the blue marker buoy to the waters and withdrawing to where the rocks were less perilous to stand on. I watched in the gathering dark – night-time pierced at the heart by piping oyster-catchers and the rapid pipistrelle of other waders – until the buoy became invisible, just as it was now, early in the morning. It was surely inevitable, as the sea sank back and I at last saw the blue buoy in the shifting slate and milky sky-reflection, that I would grow impatient to reach it, tantalized by its proximity. Hardly three or four yards out now it rose and fell. Seaweed belled up on the swell beneath it and closed again with the motion of a jellyfish, and the buoy swirled but never came to shore.

I retreated to the foreshore to find a suitable stone that would tie securely and make a weight for some spare line in my pocket, to cast towards the buoy and snag the line that tethered it. I tried of course to suspend my hope as I tugged gingerly and brought the buoy to hand. At the first short dropper the hook had been removed and the line nearby showed signs of chafing – the work of a dogfish with its tough sandpaper back? Two other hooks were gone, which gave me food for thought if nothing else to dine upon. It is one thing to fail by a tried and tested method, but a new one needs at least a gesture of encouragement from the gods. I had not had much faith in my baits and would never have used them at home. But here there were no lugworms and no ragworms I could find, only crabs and shellfish. I made cocktails of winkles, mussels and limpets, and some bits of crab, sand-wiching the more toothsome but less enduring morsels between resilient rubbery limpet.

Hope springs infernal, the better to damn you with unsuccess. Even to the last two hooks (they seemed to be snagged in weed) I still … but there, indeed, was a fish. A pollack perhaps, or an eel? No, neither, but a ling. Whatever it was I had hoped to catch, I had not expected to land a ling (or rockling, to give the name in full), still less one as long as my hand and forearm together, a beautiful russet and brown-grey fish with a yellow-milky belly, little tentacles on its snout and barbels under its chin. I had sometimes caught ling as a boy, though never of such size. But ling or leviathan, I had a method and could shower my ego with praise and have it dance a jig. What an instinct I had, what a nose for a fish, what a shipwreck survivor I was! I had yet to wait a while before I could reach my catch and still longer to untie my line but I was so elated I could only bask in the delay.

How I would enjoy now to invite you in to breakfast on fresh ling, but at what expense might such a thing be brought to the dead centre of England? A medicinal fish as folklore has it, 'a healthy fish, good for the stomach' as old Mrs Feaney at once advised me on my promising her a taste if she cared to stay. She had come over in her busy way, headscarfed, climbing the stone stile, nimble for her years, with calf muscles that would flatter a new bride, to bring me, in one hand, soda bread and, in the other, a fresh egg, a rarity I would not see again until St Patrick's Day. Her son Bartley had a roll of carpet in his loft. She wanted me to have it if I cared to fetch it and that was why she had called. It would help to keep me warm, she said. But oh no, she would not delay … having, I suppose, other fish to fry.

The Feaneys were ever concerned for my comfort. Their kindness came with a natural reserve, especially in those early days and weeks, as they studied me and formed an estimation of my character, and puzzled and probed over 'the Missus' and my 'marriage'. They would observe me so, unfailingly, with an honest eye, undiluted by sophistry, both sharp and humorous, trained to read the stranger's every move and every word and every glance. So Gregory would wait at the door when he came to say he had brought the carpet anyway, to save me, and there it was on the wall, a little stiff with the dirt of ages and more recent chicken droppings. I should beat it with a broom was his mother's advice, he said, making it plain that domestic matters were none of his domain. In my earnestness, I kept him a moment, knowing how he liked to read of an evening, and went to find a pocket edition of Synge's *The Aran Islands* I had included in my little library. He seemed pleased, I thought, or else he made the best of it. But I saw at once he would not take it there and then and so I offered to bring it with me when next I called. I wondered and wanted to know how the book might strike him.

I walked to Kilronan that day to buy a wick for an old storm lamp. It was one of those days on the island when the population seemed to have been spirited away. No one was anywhere to be seen. On my way I took my routine detour down the strand, to see if the sea had delivered any items on my tidal shopping list. Wood, floats, line, net were my most desired *trouvés*, but nothing new had been disgorged since my last inspection. I saw a school of porpoise bounding across the bay, as many as a score, I judged. They bent a little to leeward, then straightened their course back to the Sound. I thought as I watched their buoyant, frisking passage, how Melville had called them 'the lads that always live before the wind'. (I had just re-read *Moby-Dick* for the umpteenth time.) But, barring the 'lads' themselves, I did not see a soul until I reached Paul's shop, nor any coming home again, not so much as a porpoise. It was a day of almost total solitude. But I had an enviable capacity for my own society then and looked at the world before me, and neither too far forward nor too far back, except to dwell on such vital matters as the success of my night's fishing and how I might repeat and improve upon the catch. They say the fulfilment of desire is disenchantment, that presumption leads to despair, but I could see no shadow to my heart's delight that day. It is the boon of being young, an aptitude I would recover and am unable not to mourn. Who wouldn't face approaching old age and the teetering edge of life the better for it?

The storm-lamp I had found in my turf loft still had a complete glass but was rusted fairly tight. I spent much of the evening (i.e. the afternoon) getting the base to unscrew and the wick to feed and trim, and the lever to raise and to lower the glass. I love a storm lamp on the open shore. It warms the hands and warms the heart. It makes the dark swarm cosily about it and dramatizes all you do within its orbit. Besides, since low tide would be an hour later, and an hour later every night, I would need light to carry on the rocks if I was to find my cork markers and link my line to its mooring – if I was not to take a tumble on the slippery weed, break a leg perhaps or knock myself out, and lie there until the tide turned and I drowned. My line needed repairing and reinforcing but I would not touch it until I had finished with the lamp and could scrub the taint of oil and paraffin from my hands.

I took a little break and walked across the rocks to see the ocean. The choughs that chattered and wheeled on the breezes brightly through the day were homing solemnly like rooks to roost along the cliffs. Away to the south-east the great cliffs of Moher fell in a gloom of shadow. Dawn was ploughing somewhere through the distant plains to reach us again by morning. Faint stars began to prick the sky, and by the time I returned across the wide but shattered limestone pavements, figurative airstrips from which so many hearts had taken off for Boston and New York, the skyline walls were being touched with light like cooling solder. The sea swelled on the air. The air grew chill. I came down the last terrace and round by the ivy-shadowed well at a jump and a run. There I met Maggie Faherty, stooping with her pail, almost invisible in her black shawl and skirts.

It was Maggie who had ridden home in the back of McDonough's pick-up truck the evening of my arrival. Although she had two brothers living with her, I rarely saw them drawing water, and it was not that either of them was otherwise too busy hewing wood, the timber shortage being such as you know it to be. Tam was an old fisherman, a tall, lean and kindly man, with very little spoken English, though sometimes I saw him half-in, half-out of the doorway, back to the world, catching enough light in the spread of a newspaper (the English-language *Connacht Tribune*) to read by, when the light was especially dim and rain dripped from the thatch. He had a share in some lobster pots out beyond Bungowla. I would go out one perilous night to check them in his and Black Colm's company. Otherwise he did no work but milked the cow and drew the dole, while the Yank lived off his pension, upon a different plane altogether. A sister came home in the summer. She was a Yank too, come home to die, they said, of cancer. I remember her faded wiry hair, her nervous

nicotined fingers, the heels on her shoes, the myopic lipstick that
went beyond her lips, the sprawl of her American laughter. That
put four of them in the most primitive cabin in Kil-na-cer, just
across the way from me.

'No, indeed. Why would you?' said Maggie, swinging the second pail up and setting off down the narrow path, under the
fuchsia hedge. She would not have me carry the pails for her, and
so I walked as much beside her as I could, half a step before or
half a step behind, as the path twisted or the way was uneven.
Her shawled head came scarcely to my shoulder. Her hands and
wrists were thickened by a lifetime's labour. But she was spry of
manner and fiery, if content to say nothing as we went along. The
well water, looking vividly pure in the murky light, scarcely
slopped or stirred, so steady was her progress. I tried to prise her
open a crack or two.

'But tell me how many fowls do you keep? I often see you
scold them.'

'I would have a dozen if I had another,' she said at last.

'Are they good layers?'

'They are not!' she cackled wildly, 'The divil they are.' The
idea seemed to amuse her greatly.

'Do they make good eating? Do you like roast chicken?'

'You'd get more meat off a briar than any of the like of them,'
she said more pensively.

'Do you eat fish? … Do you ever eat rabbit?' I said I could
catch her a rabbit if she liked. She turned up her nose at rabbit
and we bade each other farewell at the path that led round to her
door. It was not in my nature to go out of my way to force
acquaintance. But every little step towards breaking ice naturally

pleased me (though I had broken more ice than I knew). And I thought with amusement of old Maggie as I went in to stir my fire and boil the kettle. For I could not scrub my hands without hot water, and I had no hot water on tap. Whatever you did to get by must take its time and make its space. So life on the island pursued another shape of a cruder necessity's making.

'But the night is like a day,' said Gregory, as he worked round the Big Fella, drying him off with a handful of hay, 'like a day. You will not be needing your lamp I'd say,' he laughed, amused at my enterprise, lit up, I guessed, by more than the stars. 'But good luck now,' he stood and called after me, 'good luck.'

(I heard him lead the horse away; I heard its hooves ring on the air; I heard it whinny as I went.) The night was so thick with stars, so deep and tangled with them, that even they made shadows fall. Once on the shore I lit my storm lamp nonetheless, for my pride in it, and for the warm whiff of its fumes on the sharp sea air, if nothing else. I looked for bait in its muted light among the wrack, aware as I stooped of the shadowy island about me like an island in the moon, or a star in the ocean's milky way. Seabirds and waders are as nocturnal as they are diurnal and fill the night air with their ghosting flight and piping. Their noise is a kind of aural starlight. They flicker along the breaking waves. And if the air had not been so sharp, and turning colder on the wind, I would have stayed out longer, just to hear them. But without delay I cast my blue buoy once more to the waves, took up my lamp, and left my luck to drift where it would, its baited hooks secured this time to twisted strands of steel wire. In this way I regularly caught a fish or two, a pollack, an eel, a ling, a wrasse (or, as the islanders call them, 'rockfish', always pronouncing the vowel 'o' as 'a'), until the weather broke. I liked to turn things upside down, to fish and sleep as the seas permitted and tiredness demanded, night or day. Sometimes I sat cooking my porridge and scribbling in my journal at three or four in the morning. But more often than not the winter weather ruled fishing out for several tides on end and brought my life back into kilter.

But out of kilter it was to run for a few days more regardless of the weather. For in about as much time as it takes to boil an egg, I had been branded a chicken thief by old Maggie Faherty. My chatter with her proved unhappy indeed in its timing, as six young fowls, tender pullets at the summer's end, had the day before gone missing in Kilmurvey. The old crone had seized upon my question about eating chicken and my offer of rabbit and cross-bred them, with the inevitable outcome: a cock-and-rabbit story, a species like a two-legged hare, which, once started, ran and ran before the hounds of parochial suspicion. As if to show how nature cannot tolerate a vacuum, news of our encounter now rushed before me and met me that same night in the Feaneys' kitchen. Returned from the shore, I called by to thank them for the carpet, now covering the lino in my bedroom, and to deliver Synge's book. And they told me, as if I might not know, that I had met old Maggie, whom they regarded with fond humour, and how she had said I had offered her fish to eat, and rabbit, and … chickens. I laughed with them about her and marvelled at her spirit, but I did not think to correct her version of the story.

I had no inkling of the case against me until Gregory later told me of its dismissal. But I soon became aware of something at the time that seemed to pass for a posting to Coventry. Michael Gill and his wife Kathleen, whose missing fowls stood or flew at the centre of the drama, suddenly began to cut me when I met them on the road. It was no minor matter for them to have lost so many birds at a swoop. Even to have lost one would have been more than enough to bear, in a land where a fresh egg is almost as rare as one of gold. What a low and barefaced villain I must have seemed, what an insolent fiend, brazenly hailing old Mrs Gill as she made her way to Conneely's shop along the narrow puddled lane (to buy perhaps an egg?). It was seldom clear as you approached her, with her paradoxically small, wire-framed spectacles that drew their opaque lenses goggle-like across her nose, whether she recognized you or not. To add to your confusion, she had an odd way of carrying her head half-tilted to the sky. But she recognized me all right and turned from the sight of me, resolutely, and passed me on the other side, which is to say scarcely six feet away.

There was more to it than just the cut that was affecting. Something about her uncommon bulk, her bandaged leg and cautious progress, seemed, in the great bare and sky-filled world about us, that awful moral landscape, to add a depressing pathos to the moment. She clutched her shopping bag before her and stepped between the puddles like an adventuring mother hen. What was it I had done? Given mortal offence to Michael with my idle playboy manners? I could not begin to guess and chose to dismiss the old lady's behaviour as pure crankiness, produced perhaps by the onset of winter, until Michael treated me similarly, down at the corner by the bay. I believe I saw him flinch too, but he stuck to his guns and blankly refused me the time of day. But then the fowls reappeared and returned to their owners, having managed, it was thought, to get themselves shut up overnight in someone's outbuilding.

It had come on to rain and blow again. Although never a day went by without my taking some turn in it, life tended to go to ground when the wind blew up so high that it could punch a wall flat at a blow. I read and wrote and even set myself exercises to try to improve the balance of my sentences. (*La lotta continua* …) I loitered at my own or at the Feaneys' hearth. I engaged in Crusoevean husbandries or scribbled in my journal:

*Sunday, 10 November … One moment here starlings are burbling in the thatches, the sparrows are chattering, and there's sunlight asparkle in the puddles. The people open their doors and loiter more. Out on the rocks rainwater from the night before trickles through the fluted terraces and gullies. It is like a day of thaw. Goldfinches loop among the dwellings, threading extraordinary trinkets of colour through varieties of grey. A charm of goldfinches, they say. I think of them crossing the Sound, or can they be residents? I am not ornithologist enough to know. I guess they pass down the islands into Clare, and up the islands from that direction, the crossings that way being far narrower, but don't know. I hate not knowing facts. By late evening the rocks tighten into the greyness of themselves and grow more bleak, without visible light relief of lichen or mineral. The blackbirds, humped among the rocks, sound their customary alarms (I think incongruously of suburban gardens at nightfall, of deciduous shadows). And now if they rise to fly they're snatched away by the wind. We're set for a wild night. Already my door is rattling and the house moaning and complaining. The timbered kitchen creaks. I have three-quarters of a bucket of coal left. Half a ton promised for delivery tomorrow. So I'm burning far more driftwood than coals and have made a damper from a board I found this evening on Kilmurvey shore. With dogged sawing I have cut it so that it slots between the bottom of the bowed basket of the fire itself and the stone floor. It cuts off direct updraft and keeps the ash from spilling out. It has charred a little but doesn't yet threaten to ignite. The wood is hard and soused and I could hardly saw it, not helped by grazing my knuckles when the blade caught and buckled and sang with a kind of cartoon boi-oi-oi-oing. Immediately you with-draw it the wood flares up and when you slip it back again the fire fades. It's a perfect innovation in the interests of both economy and cuisine.*

*Monday, 11 November. Cuisine? My culinary skills leave too much to be desired to begin remotely to legitimate the term. I fry. I parboil and fry. I mash potato by the mountain and boil vegetables: carrots, turnip, onions. I mash them all together. I fry up the cold leavings as bubble-and-squeak. I bake a potato in the fire. A boiled onion and fresh fish fried in butter is a house speciality. I make porridge no one could fault, except for the issue of salt, too little or too much according to your taste. I make a dreadful stew. How do you make it thicken? Tonight it will be the last mutton chop. (6/– of meat on Saturday. I walked there. A family of redheads, as meat purveyors might be.) I went to Conneely's shop. Bill for: 3 pks soup, 1/2 a pound of butter, 1 pk porridge oats (14/– 'on account of the double freight'). Double freight they say is imposed on all goods for the duration of the steamer's absence. Seems opportunistic to me. My coal came and that's the chief concern of the day, a bitingly raw day. They left the sacks upon the wall. All heavy with wet but there was good sound coal among the sludge of slack. £14 a ton, or have I said? (The rest next week, he said.) I humped them in until my hands turned black and blue with coal-dust and cold. It rained hard throughout with icy rain and soaked me through. I've had a bonanza since, a regular blaze, and tonight I plan a bath, in an old tin bath, before the flames. I'm drying out some sacks to use against the rain that's driving hard beneath the door. It's the wildest night I think I've ever known. The candles shudder and lunge, the gas globe labours. Somewhere a horse is loose upon the road, they say, but you'd hardly hear it coming for the massed hooves of the wind. I sometimes start from my page thinking someone's banging at the door...*

*Tuesday, 12 November. Dole day wild and black as Guinness, legless as an ocean ... we had a lull this evening when I thought the wind was going to die but it was just shifting its bearings. The sea is up so high about the island you can easily imagine you're voyaging, lunging on to America. I've been out to see how the bay looks (choked to the neck with weed) but I'm on my last dry pair of trousers (one pair yesterday coal heaving, one pair again carelessly today along the strand, getting caught by a wave while struggling to drag a spar from among the weed). I scribble. I read much. I prowl, restlessly mooching from window to window, making observations, or looking for anything to observe. From the gable window in the loft I can look right down the island but nothing moves except the rain which blurs what there is to see. The margins of the house are cold and draughty. In the lean-to filling a kettle I peep through the low window to catch by chance old Maggie emerging. As if in a mime of violent storm, she edges out against the weight of the wind, heaves the door shut behind her. (Hens must keep indoors.) She goes just down the side of the cabin a step only, leans back against the wall, hoiks up her skirts in a bunch behind and pisses (evidently no drawers) ...*

There was talk at the Feaneys' at nightfall of the loss of an island trawler some time that morning, but Gregory was not back to give ballast to the rumour. The story gradually filled itself out in the next few days. Opinion was clear that the crew to whom the boat had been entrusted were too young. It was, I heard the woman at the post office say, 'folly lucky not to be a tragedy', in one of those startling locutions with which bilingualism can be so perfectly inspired. The weather was too fierce for them and they were lucky they were not drowned. The sooner the steamer returned the better, for now there was only one boat in it to bring supplies from Connemara. 'No eggs to spare,' they'd tell me time and again at the shop. (I always appreciated that 'to spare'; it told me so plainly where I stood in the pecking order.) Who knew but 'double freight' might yet itself be doubled. By Sunday, when I went over to supper at the Feaneys' table, Gregory had obtained a report of the incident, torn from the *Connacht Tribune*. Even before we sat down, and we were late, as Mary chided, Gregory took the cutting from behind the clock, unfolded it and read it for my benefit (I reproduce it from the yellow cutting itself, as glued into my journal, with original spelling and punctuation and without Mary's libellous interruptions and commentary):

FISHERMEN LOSE FIGHT
TO SAVE TRAWLER FROM
STORM OFF ARAN

*The Aran islands fishing trawler* Ard Aengus *owned by Mr Gregory Conneeley of Kilronan one of the best-known fishermen on the west coast was wrecked in heavy seas off the south coast of Inishmore on Tuesday while being towed to Kilronan. Earlier that morning the 75 foot vessel worth £30,000 and built about five years ago had been fish-*

*ing off Mutton Island on the Clare Coast with 28 year old Thomas Conneeley of Kilronan as skipper and two companions John Michael Gill of Kilronan and John Faherty of Oldquarter, Inishmore, both in their 20s.*

*The propeller shaft became fouled by a cable and the vessel started to drift. The Galway based trawler* Star of Faith *skippered by Mr Pat Jennings of Long Walk went to the assistance of the* Ard Aengus *but efforts to free the propeller failed and the* Star of Faith *took her in tow.*

*The weather deteriorated as they neared the islands and while passing between Inishmaan and Inishmore in Gregory Sound the tow rope broke and the trawler which had a lot of gear still out began to drift. Her owner-skipper took out his brother John's trawler the* Ard Colm *and went to help the* Star of Faith. *They got a chain aboard the stricken trawler but the wind was gusting to Force 8 and 9 and after a short while the chain broke and the three crewmen were taken off as the vessel grounded near Glassin Rocks. An Aran fisherman who saw the salvage efforts said there was no hope of salvage once the chain tow broke and the vessel was wrecked swiftly. He said the crew were lucky to be alive. Over 20 years ago 15 fishermen from the village of Killeany on the same part of the coast were drowned close to the point where the trawler grounded. The area was being swept by westerly gale gusts reaching 80mph at times on Tuesday night and all hopes of salvaging anything from the wreck were abandoned.*

'Eighty miles an hour,' exclaimed Gregory with a whistle as he set to the fish before him.

''Twas never twenty years ago but a hundred, more like,' came Mary's parting shot.

'Newspapers never get facts right,' I said, giving them the benefit of my professional wisdom.

To dine off salt-cured wrasse, a traditional island dish – in this instance a gift to the Feaneys from a resident of Bungowla – might remind you of nothing more than Charlie Chaplin making a methodical meal of his boot. For wrasse are tacked together by numerous short, thick bones, like cobbler's nails. Their meat is almost as thin on the bone as you'd find it to be on the nails of even a well-heeled boot. No matter how long you soak it and rinse it, once cured it tastes for ever of the salt-sea. Only an ocean of spring water might quench the thirst it gives you. And so there we sat before it, subdued, all thought of conversation gone. Heads sinking, hearts sunk to the bottom of the sea, speechless to the last bone, we suffocated and drowned in a tedium of bones, scales like miniature pantiles, and salt by the pillar. It was a penance, not a feast, and the plate before me, with its neatly arranged border of bones, seemed an offering to the gods, to save the fishing fleet from extinction. No wonder the lighthouse-keeper had gone so overboard about his goose.

# 5

## *Solitude and Sea Pie*

The island's winter storm-wakes sometimes brought fog, and
then solitude seemed to intensify in the attendant muffled silence
that amplified the crash and back-roar of the sea. You heard the
sea as clear as crystal but heard much more the silence that
enveloped it and enveloped you. Enormous silence carried you on
straining ears, stumbling at the end of the world, listening for
landfall, dreaming of the tolling bell. It was like the end of the
world when fog came down. Your mind becalmed seemed to
creak and echo hollowly under its oppression. You could think
yourself anywhere beyond Finistère and Malin Head, looking for
Hy-Brasil or Atlantis, or Cape Cod or Nantucket. You must feel
your way home, or search for it still deeper in the submarine fog
induced by Guinness. You must light the lamp and skulk indoors
and dry your clothes before the fire. You must retreat. You must
sink down, to a kind of crustacean consciousness. But what you
wanted was to be outside, harvesting seaweed or, in my case, jet-

sam, newly disgorged on the landward shore to supplement my coals.

We had many field days along the strand as the year sank down, by shorter and shorter strides, to the foot of dank December, when grey puddles swam in the lane and the turlough behind the bay filled and stayed, an inland haunt for the half-spent light of winter. Weed rolled man-deep in the waves and broke their fall, making the sea seem oily and slow, though it ran clear as aerated spring water through the tangled yellow-brown, red-brown fronds, and claw-footed limbs, and all the detritus of shipboards that would dry in the tide-mark among the weed and sand, or jam among the rocks that edged the bay, to be smoothed and shaped and salt-dried. The taste of brine and weed hung on the air in heavy concentrations, and dripped from the ocean fog. Distilled, you might say, it lay limpid at low tide, preserving sea-anemones among the finer weeds and barnacles, and other dormant rock-pool specimens. Had you woken to find salt on your lips and seaweed draped about your bed and fishes in your piss-pot, it would hardly have surprised you at such times. Three days and nights, three days and nights, as the fisherman said, with a dead man in a curragh, soused by the mobile mineral sea. The mewling gull roosts overhead adrift upon your chimney. Wake and listen to your heartbeat, full fathom five, among the island's innumerable drowned. Think of all the monuments to drowned fishermen along the roadsides, looking out to sea.

The survivors, for so they were, came down to the shore to gorge on the glut of weed. Homespun men, and men in miscellaneous trousers and jackets of worn-out Sunday bests, under napless peaked caps, berets and bonnets, with their mythic weed-draped dromedaries, sealed in the noise of the sea, they overlapped history, as the waves overlapped and coughed up their kelp with a crump and a long inhalation. Squelching stalks and foliage about their boots, raking and forking with their tines like beardless Neptunes, their collective motto seemed to be: 'Seaweed for the cultivation of roots.' Rootedness, I liked to think, was what I most desired, for all that I had so impatiently uprooted myself, for we all have roots, whatever the mix of the soil. I prized it, anyway, in the island people. Their stoical lives seemed to chasten me and I wanted to live as they did. Community, however damaged, is the angel of locality. Sometimes on the island still, as at even these latter-day free-for-all weed gatherings, its spirit triumphed over necessity and exile. You had always to think when looking on the people there how familiar they were with each other from childhood, how interwoven all their worlds, how intimate, no matter that those worlds had broken and were still breaking up, as all worlds always are, but seldom so dramatically, on such an open stage, under the wide roof of the Atlantic sky.

By far my best find at that time was the head of an old fork, discovered not by the sea but among rocks and undergrowth behind my house. I saw its purpose at a glance, and once I had banged the soil and the rotten timber of the shaft from its socket I put it to its use, across the basket of my fire. There at the full height and centre of the fire, it enabled me to balance three pots or pans in a row without danger of them tilting and spilling as the coals subsided. It made the pots more efficient, too, by keeping them clear of tar. When my coals were especially low and I didn't want to wait for new fuel to ignite and burn, I could take the benefit of the embers by inserting the fork between the lower bars and thereby bring the kettle quicker to the boil. I found as well thrown up on the shore a square of hardboard which I used in combination with my damper board, to make my fire roar. By tailoring it a little and securing it across the open fire, braced behind a length of fishing cord slung between two nails, and removing the damper I'd constructed already, I could create a fierce updraft that made the dullest embers spark and flare. As the furnace roared it seemed to suck in air beneath the door and with it blow the starlings round the wintry sky to cool their toes. In this way I made the most of my coals and firewood, burning no more than a bucket of coal a day, except on wash days, bath days, and days of bitter weather. I consciously thought that I made the most of myself too, given the circumstances, in that dimension of life that thrives upon inventive making and patient making do, the little rhythms of simple domesticity. Often through my stay, on raw mornings, as I felt its cold metal rust-pocked haft, or at porridge hour or other cooking times, as I took a cloth in my hand to move the grill it made nearer the heat or farther from it, I relished the plain utility of my discovery.

I also disentangled from the carnage on the strand four orange marker-buoys and a broken lobster pot, and kept these by as the purest boon for future piscatorial adventures. But already I was short of line, through suffering so many early losses, and as yet could only dream of fishing five lines in the one night's tide. The repair of the lobster pot would require wire and the discovery of pliable wood. It was of a barrel shape and caved in at one end. I could see it reconstructed in my mind's eye and knew where I would leave it, at the farthest margin of the tide, for lobster or for crab – I wouldn't be choosy. But for now it smelled so strongly of the sea that I put it in the pigsty. I built my shrines of timber too, and piecemeal retrieved them from the shore until I had as much as I could care to house, with a few still-resinous props of pine and hefty planks laid out upon bare bedsprings in the end room, a wooden wake, a sacrifice awaiting the saw and consignment to the flames. The first frosts of the winter made fossil and fern patterns on the panes, inside and out, and the house stood cold just a yard back from the hearth. The chasm of my kitchen drew the heat away at once and killed it dead. When the weather turned muggy and close, the rain took less than a day to sop the sacks I used to keep it out and ran across the kitchen floor from front to back.

I look back with some incredulity at those days most of all, between what you could hardly call the honeymoon of my arrival and my eventual establishment, or half-awkward standing, among my hosts. I was the archetypal uninvited stranger. They called me, in the Irish idiom, 'the stranger'. That was both to each other and to my face, whenever I met two or more of them and my business came into discussion. It was natural to the people's usage but being unfamiliar to mine I was amused to feel its weight the more. Otherwise I was 'mister' and 'sir' or 'the gentleman', but, at least, never 'your honour', I am pleased to say. Several weeks would go by before the Feaneys used my first name, but that was a matter of old-world manners and reciprocated shynesses. Still more time passed before I could begin to accompany Gregory about his work, or help the family, wallpapering a bedroom (together with the schoolmaster), or clipping the privet hedge (a bit of a disaster). Although I planned to connive at working in the fields with Gregory and Bartley, I was content enough for now to let things fall out as they would. If I must subsist on a verbal diet of 'Fine evening' exchanged upon the road, of 'God to you' and 'God and Mary to you', with a little gossip at the Feaneys' hearth thrown in, or an occasional audience with Michael Gill, then so I would.

The unspoken part of my days was as huge as the windblown sky above. And so it was for many islanders too. We all lived in a solitude that seemed to darken the heart as winter took its hold, and days grew short, and nights were long. One man at Kil-na-cer, in his early thirties at most, living alone in the new bungalow, never spoke a word to me from November to October, though we often met upon the road and, if I did not call a greeting, I nearly always nodded to him, or gestured with beseeching glances, ready to nod, in the willing way that you do. In fact I rarely saw him detained with anyone for more than the briefest of exchanges. It seemed to me he lived a life of terrible intensity and inexplicable urgency, haring off down the island every day in a kind of madness. Such lives were conditioned not just by weather and wilderness, solitude and, in most cases, material poverty, but by relentless poverty of prospect too. Hence, for most of the older and settled people, the necessity of their ardent faith, the kneeling in the road before the cross, as I had vividly seen, the endless ill-afforded donations in small envelopes to St Martin of Porres, the promises of priests, the need to invest in some other world, beyond even America, to get by.

Little wonder then that I, reticent by nature, born into the Protestant tradition (though I've always scorned all organized forms of religion) and such a very young man, with a wife, or what was it amiss there? following what business precisely? – should need time to come into his own, whatever his own might prove to be. It's easy not to realize how very young a person is at twenty-two, when you're the person concerned. As I write this now, I contemplate my son approaching that age. He's not half the fool I was, I'm afraid to say.

One Sunday, in those early days, I made a new acquaintance. Finding myself in Kilronan after a long walk across the island, down the lanes from the village of Gort na gCapall (garden, or meadow, of the horses), I was drawn by a gathering crowd (relatively speaking, a crowd) to the village hall and went in to see the pictures showing there: some documentary footage about life in England after the war, with impeccably manicured Ealing Studios voice-over. This quaint performance was followed by Hollywood in the persons of Tom and Jerry and, as the big feature, Glenn Ford starring in *The Sheepman*. Than which what better choice in an island noted for its feuds, its large-boned creamy ewes, and its cottage industry of knitting? When at last in that film the hero shot the villain, the audience rattled their chairs and cheered with delight, before dispersing home on foot, far and near, under the windswept stars. But I found I could not suspend my disbelief or sit for long without thinking of the wilderness outside as backdrop to what flashed and flickered on the screen.

By chance as we left I fell in with Dara Flaherty. A short, lean man with spectacles, a French beret, and an eager, intelligent face, he seemed deliberately to catch my eye and said hello. He lived not far from Oatquarter. In the summer we would often meet to fish, on the low Atlantic rocks below the high cliffs of Blind Sound, in the long shadow of Dún Aengus. He had been out of Aran many years and seen the world, as so many had. Although it amused him to hear of my adventure, he took it in his stride. We spoke about the recent trawler accident – it was on the lips of all the world: 'and not so much as a splinter found'. Inevitably, it seemed, he told me of the 1852 disaster when fifteen men from Killeany were dashed against the rocks by a wave and drowned. And at once, as he pushed his bike beside me up the high hill road, he recited a song, as he called it, a pious little monody it proved, written by a visiting priest, to commemorate the tragedy. He later copied the poem for me. I have it now beside me as I received it, on four blue, lined sheets of writing paper, held together by a pin, and, with the help of a literal translation, I have since made out this version:

YOUNG-GRASSES ROCK

I

One autumn morning
When all was sweet
No malice in the wind or air,
The glorious sun
Shone warm and genial,
Gently disposed
To the whole wide world.

II

It was the feast of Glorious Mary,
The year of 1852,
When a crowd of young men,
Bold and quick,
Went fishing at
Young-grasses Rock.

III

They saw a great mound
Moving near them,
Easy and lazy,
A clumsy sea-monster:
A powerful wave
That now bore boldly down.

IV

Nor did they think as need was
To make it from the shore
But tended to their tackle
Till the rocks ran with a roar,
And met the power
Of the leaping wave.

V

Alas! was no escaping
The vile wild wave that hung
Heavy on high above the rocks,
And all the brave men doomed
Upon the flagstones drowned.

VI

Its power now bent and broken
Upon the flagstones bare,
The wave sank home:
My thousand sorrows' care
But it went not empty.

VII

For it swept upon the fierce edge
Fifteen men in the flower of bravery,
Leaving sorrow and tears
And heartbreak to
The people of Killeany.

VIII

Sorrow and torment
In Killeany that day,
As fathers, mothers
And loving relations,
Mournful and demented,
Wept and lamented,
Keening the strong men
Who'd never return.

IX

Early they rose that morning
Cheerful and strong,
Filled with hope
And light of heart,
But to lay happiness
Upon a bier
Before night fell.

X

O here is a sign to heed,
To judge not what is before us
Or put our souls in pawn,
For we must save the harvest
Before our hour be flown.

XI

Who knows in what place
Or on what shore
Death will come
To sweep him on his way?
So must we be upon our guard
And ready for the day.

XII

That tragedy our lesson
Swift and sudden
Upon Young-grasses Rock,
Their souls swept to heaven
Lost in the sleep of life.

When he had told it to me once, he told it to me again, translating and glossing each line as he went, halting on the hill to comment. He spoke it with a dying rhythm in a keening nasal tone that my uneven, artless version fails entirely to recapture, although I understand the original to be also wanting in art.*

*The Times* of London carried the following report on the 'Melancholy Catastrophe', posted Galway, Tuesday evening, in its issue of Friday, 20 August 1852: 'Yesterday [which would date the incident 16 August, though it is usually recorded as having occurred on 15 August] a most calamitous circumstance occurred in one of the islands of Arran [sic] by which 15 unfortunate men have been swept away from time into eternity in a single moment. All of them were fishing with lines on a cliff when notwithstanding the weather was calm a sudden wave broke over the cliff on which they were standing and washed them out into the deep. Only four of the bodies have been found up to last night. Many of the poor fellows had left large families to mourn over the irreparable loss. A subscription has already been set on foot, and it is hoped a large sum will be raised for them, now that Galway is so crowded with nobility and gentry of the United Kingdom.'

'Never trust the sea,' he said, 'there's the lesson in it, even on dry land.'

The priest's homiletic designs didn't seem to impose on him at all. But Dara was a sceptic, of sorts.

'The Man of Aran? You know what you can do with the Man of Aran,' he once scoffed, complaining to me, as we stood before the ocean, at the corner of the Sound, how his wife had tried to dissuade him from his fishing to go into Kilronan for a showing of Flaherty's famous film.

'Fuck the Man of Aran,' he said.

We used to fish on the low ledges as the tide came in, exposed to the sea's vagaries, though never to more than a large seventh roller, just like those fifteen men. But then that night we reached the brow and he swung astride his bike and sailed off down the road. It was a perishing night, above a restless, roaring sea. The wind brightened the stars and my nose and ears until they too shone and rang with cold.

For myself I agree with the man who said that the only religious act we can securely perform is to wash ourselves well. I normally conducted my devotions with a kettle of hot water and a jug of cold over an old-fashioned washstand before my bedroom window. On Sunday mornings, as I stood there shivering naked, looking out at the day over the half of net curtain, I would sometimes see the Feaneys ride by bound for Mass. Raised on the side-car, just above the wall, they went aslant as the Big Fella took them carefully down the little hill, Gregory in his best jacket and cap, Mrs Feaney and Mary in their newest headscarves, a blanket about their knees. They seemed the image and epitome of stability and familial devotion. They once struck up a commotion just past my house where a neighbour had two pigs in one of the gardens. The horse wouldn't pass the pigs, as is common with horses where pigs are concerned, especially squealing pigs. It reared up and backed away, giving Mrs Feaney and Mary a rocky time. In the end they had to dismount and Gregory had to lead the horse on. But even that required a lot of oaths in Irish before they could get off to commune with their god.

My more solemn observances were also taken weekly, in the tin bath. There I would huddle before my maker, knees up by my ears, feet out or feet in, shins scorching, back chill, until driven to disembark and turn about. Or, grinding the bath round, water slopping, I'd go port or starboard on, and, getting briefly comfortable, soak a while and meditate upon my new-found lot or merely stare into the fire, listening to the wind about the house, the little cymbal tinkling at my door, the mice adventuring in the loft. Or if conditions were favourable I'd tune my ailing radio to some talk or music.

What was I doing there? It sometimes needed to be asked. Ostensibly I had come to see what it was like and how the people lived upon the island, not in the easy tourist season but at the worst time of the year. I'd come for more obscure reasons too, to put the world behind me and the glib hot-air talk of educated work, to test myself against solitude and hardship. I had not come believing I might stay forever, though now and then I wondered how I might contrive to. 'But avoid introspections,' I wrote in my journal, 'keep on the outside. The world is all outside to be seen'; and I might have pencilled it on my whitewashed chimney-breast along with my hearthstone's questionable epigraph – 'The mass of men lead lives of quiet desperation' – had I been so bold.

One night, quite late in December (my journal shows me it was Friday, 20 December), my bathing rites were disturbed. I'd stood up and was dripping in mid-manoeuvre when I heard voices and several people – I couldn't say how many – jumping my stile and seeming to surge towards my door. I had neither lamp nor candle lit to suggest I was at home, only an outsize fire burning. I stepped as I was into my trousers, dragged a sweater over my head and squirmed into my boots. In my urgency I banged against a chair I'd set beside the bath and knocked my radio into the tub. It was playing through a gauze of interference an orchestral concert, transmitted I believe from Dublin. I snatched it out but not before the seeds of fatal damage were sown. I crossed and stood at an angle to the window to see, without stirring the curtain, what lay in store for me outside. But the firelight was strong enough to obscure the night against the glass. After a studied attempt at silence, broken by murmurings and whisperings, they – whoever they were – rapped at my door.

I stood upon a chair and lit my lamp and called, 'Come in'. I had by now guessed they were a benign party, for most of the voices sounded youthful and were suddenly very audibly accompanied by cowbells. They pushed the door wide and a crowd of young red faces surged forward. At their head a young boy proffered a china pig for money. Then at some signal that escaped me they began at once to sing in Irish a Christmas carol of what I considered to be unusual duration. From the volume they produced it was clear there were several more of them and some adults gathered in the garden. I looked out what change I had and duly pressed the coins into the back of the pig as they sang, then stepped to stand before my bath, peculiarly wishing to hide it from view. The singers' faces looked oddly immobile beyond their mouths, but their eyes swept eagerly about the room and held me under close inspection. We stared at each other, I smiling encouragement, and they singing earnestly, edging further into the room and beginning to look more freely about them. It was indeed a carol of uncommon length and both performers and audience began to feel the strain of it. I didn't know where to look, and they began to get distracted from their words, to stumble and to mouth out of time with the more resolute, older voices outside. Then they stopped singing as abruptly as they had begun, *in medias res* as it seemed, and shuffled backwards into the night. I went to the door and called aloud, 'Thank you very much', and was met by a chorus of 'HAPPY CHRISTMAS' that might have been heard by the stars. I stood in my damp clothes and listened to them as they went around the village, singing at every home.

Christmas was coming but if the goose was getting fat I had no prospective share in it. Neither had I plans nor inkling as to how I would pass the festivities. Would they be the first I'd spend on my own? And why not just ignore it, if I was anything of the philosopher I aspired to be? I thought that I would dine on rabbit, having by now perfected a method of taking them through the drystone wall above Kilmurvey Bay. The rabbits had their burrows in the last steep field that ran down to the road beside the bay. At night they slipped through the gaps in the bottom of the wall and went to graze in the long fields back towards the village, a plague in a country where green was so rare a shade. Their runs were plain to see, enabling me to reduce those with access through the wall to three or four by plugging the surplus gaps with rocks. Then round about midnight, when even the latest late-night drinker was likely to be snoring, far adrift, and no one was around to stumble on me, I'd make a circuit from our village through the back end of Kilmurvey, past the ball alley, and down onto the road, to walk back towards the bay. I'd jump the wall beside the bay and, locating the gaps I'd left, set a purse net in the mouth of each. (A purse net is a device like a string bag on a drawstring. You poke the bottom part of the mouth of the net through onto the floor of the hole with a stick. Then you spread the rest of the net, tethering it by hooking its meshes on points and angles of the stone and pinning it lightly into position with little sticks. The end of the drawstring is tethered to a stake or, where the topsoil is thin, you tie it as I did around a boulder. My father had taught me such nefarious tricks in my boyhood.)

I was always elaborately cautious not to leave my scent or otherwise to scare my supper. So I walked back the way I had come, stopping off at home to steam my porridge and take a cup of coffee and maybe scribble a little, before going out again, at about two in the morning, to approach my nets from the Kilmurvey end. I walked zig-zag as fast as I could through first one field then the other, driving as I hoped my supper before me. Had I been more fond of their flesh I might have made a serious impact on the local rabbit population. But I took one only once in a while, to vary my menu, or fill a gap, when the bacon I now ordered up from Galway failed to get through, when the weather was also too wild to fish, and the butcher's meat was finished for the week.

So I toyed with the idea of rabbit for Christmas. But then next morning I received my invitation to join the Feaneys at their table. I looked forward to nothing more. I went off to Kilronan, straight away, to buy in a bottle or two of drink that I might bring to oil the occasion. With two and nearly three months behind me now, I began at last to feel at home. In response to this feeling, or as an expression of it, finding little attraction in the 'hurly-burly' of Kilronan and the lure of its dim lights, I had already started, unconsciously at first, to keep my orbits local. If I walked, I found I walked westwards. Then deliberately, on into the spring, I began to say that if I ever went to Kilronan again I'd never do so more than once a month. I pledged my hours to the wilderness.

If I went a circuit for the day with my kindling and folding frying pan, my quarter of soda bread, my rashers and my Heinz baked beans, my wedge of Galtee processed cheese, I rose early and travelled at my leisure to the west, either along the landward shore, to Lough Dearg and on beyond, clambering and ventur-ing, back-tracking here and there the better to advance around the rocky storm-beach, or outward by Dún Aengus and the cliffs, until I made the shore to the west below Bungowla, hard by the ocean or the Sound. There are really only three settlements between Kil-na-cer and Bungowla – Sruffaun, the village of Onaght, and Craggancareen – and I bypassed them all in going on my way. Nor need I set foot in Bungowla itself, coming round by the long low fields to the north, where the shore runs green and the sea can seem to lap like a lake across to Connemara. I did not care to. I craved the empty seaborne world as if it were a heaven. I cannot say I cared nothing for the weather, for the weather was more than integral to all there was: it was most of what there was, giving character to sky and sea and stone. If the day blew wild I felt different from when it was calm, just as I progressed differently, of that there's no denying, but either way I took things as they came and welcomed the variety. Let it pick me to pieces as if I was inanimate, by still fine rain or by the teeth of the wind. I loved nothing more than to tuck myself in among the rocks with a bit of driftwood and cook my snack. No such thing as a cooked snack was needed but I made one the focus of my day, the fire at the heart of it, beside the greater fire of the sea.

Only at the edge of the world can you see what a cambered and containing place earth is, how everything is somehow hooped about it, and within it. Here the passage of a black-backed gull bent upon the wind, the plummet of a peregrine, the white sea horses galloping to or from America, or the gyrations of a stoat threading in and out among the boulders and rocks, as if it tried to hold me mesmerized, might be all the life I'd see, except for the life that light leads, in sea or in stone, making even grey disintegrate and scatter into colour. Travel now at once, if you doubt me, and sail to the island. There sit out and search for anything that is or stays a single colour and is not atomized into an entire spectrum by the falling ocean light.

Sometimes when the sea was boisterous and I was looping back along the cliffs, wall-hopping along the dizzy edge from Lough Murvey to Dún Aengus, I'd go a little further out of my way to the jumble of rocks to seaward of Gort na gCapall and walk along to see the sea glug up and down and spray out spume in Poll na bPeist (worm or serpent hole), the deep and perfectly rectangular trough, like a swimming pool, as everyone remarks, that lay cut, by some bizarre geological freak, in the broad ledge beside the open Atlantic. Returning from the hole after such a day's vigorous adventure, a gloomy mixed bag of a day, the Sunday before Christmas Eve, I happened on a scene that led me to disaster. I had never walked straight across the island at its narrowest point before, so tempted by the novelty I cut across the desert rock into the gloaming, among the walls and crevices and glacial boulders, until I could lower myself down into the boreen that ran from Gort na gCapall to the bay at Kilmurvey. By now I was thinking warmly of home, of starting my fire and settling in, as I came along the high-walled track and round where the fields fell more openly to view. The light had almost thinned away to nothing but still veered in the turlough among the little flock of waders – oyster-catchers, sandpipers – and gulls that shrilled and whistled and harried there throughout the months of middle winter. Rain spat on the gusting breeze and shadows now grew fast below the walls and spread towards the water, touching it with a last brief intensity of light along one shore.

It was then I noticed the two men. They eased themselves over the wall, away down by the road. Any figure in the landscape would have held my attention, for I had been a day without sight of a single soul. But these two passed guns between them as they climbed into the field. So I drew back in the shadows and watched them as they came, stalking, half stooping, towards the birds about the turlough. They had no real cover and were forced to shoot as the birds began to stir and wheel in little restless arcs that touched the ground or water, only to leave again, in an instant, as if upon some current of electricity. The men fired two barrels each and then a fifth shot, wildly it seemed, into the shrill cloud as it swept in confusion about the water, above the rocks, and away to the safety of the shore. The gunshots resounded briefly before being snaffled by the air. Three or four birds lay dead or flapping in the shallow water. A single wounded oyster-catcher limped and fluttered away.

The men picked up and despatched their prey but did not seem to have seen where the wounded bird had gone to. They wandered up and down a while. I heard their voices muffled on the breeze. Night had almost fallen and it was hard to pick out the men until they moved, or make out boulder or wall from field and water. Even the water had sunk into the dark. I had kept my eye upon the oyster-catcher and taken a fix on the boulder by which I had seen it last, fifty or more yards away. I leant back in by the wall and waited. A burst of rain blew across and fell a while and at last the men retired. But I waited until they must be well upon their way before I climbed into the field. I had to cir-cle the water in the dark and find my way to where I could – or could I? – pick out the boulder behind which I thought the wounded bird had gone to hide.

I located what I believed was the rock but the bird was nowhere to be found. I walked a little farther on and strained my eyes to see. I took a few steps more and then turned back and walked in another direction from the boulder, to the far wall, and so on, and round, tenaciously, all but blind. I returned to the boulder and upon an impulse felt round it in the grass and dis-covered about its base little crannies and hollows where the grass was inaccessible to grazing beasts, and that was where I found the broken creature, with splayed wing and bent neck, its long bill nose down in the grass. It didn't so much as move as I picked it up. There was, however, just life left in it and so, knowing the shock of what had befallen it would kill it even were its bodily wounds to mend, I tapped its head on the rock and slipped it into my pocket.

By common standards oyster-catcher or sea-pie is no delicacy. But by my standards at that time the promise of fresh meat, however small the morsel, was a promise to anticipate with pleasure. Why else had the men come down to shoot, even on the Lord's day? Weren't we all in a similar, if not the same, boat? I had wondered, I must say. The curlew, when it has been upon the moor from spring to summer's end, can seem almost as tasty as grouse. But once it has wintered a few weeks on the shore, the flesh turns saline. There had been no curlews at the turlough, the curlew being a wily and watchful creature, but these smaller shoreline waders would be no different case, I knew. I don't believe the oyster-catcher ever strays far or for long from the vicinity of the sea. It nests among the pebbles and its long cry never mingles with the even longer limpid note of the curlew away in the sedgy-peat-moss salt-free air and water of the uplands. I knew all this but still I savoured the prospect of my sea-pie.

The word 'oyster' alone, of course, makes people nod sagely. Sometimes I forget how ill I felt, how feverish, how I could keep nothing inside me, how tender and painful; and, knowing how devious our subconscious manoeuvres can be, I have even doubted I was that ill at all. But I was more than ill enough not to trust to luck. By the time the nurse arrived – there was no doctor – it was the eve of Christmas Eve. I swear that when she leant over me, pressing my abdomen, asking did it ever hurt me here (yes), or here (yes), I could smell alcohol on her breath – a drop of something seasonal taken somewhere on the way, but hardly inspiring of confidence, unless I was hallucinating. 'Running a temperature,' she said, and put on her gloves. Tightening the belt on her blue gabardine, snapping her bag shut, an odd, portly figure she cut, with a face and eye that even in the failing twilight of my room reminded me of a Christmas turkey, its wattles full of faintly purple blood. She said she thought it would be wise to go into hospital in Galway. As good luck had it, so she judged, the steamer would come out in the morning, returning to Galway by the islands.

What would you have done? I agreed to go. It was my fortune's lowest ebb. But I remembered how cousin Norman had died of neglected peritonitis, out on a remote Galloway holding. I recalled the story of the uncle in that same country, gored by a bull. He suffered so much pain he tore his mattress to shreds, and died before help arrived, to enter the family rattlebag of horror stories. It was not as though the hazards of living in remote, inaccessible places were not well documented. Done to death by an oyster-catcher? It seemed inglorious. If I must go, I tried to joke, I would go with a little more style than that. But in truth I was ill that night and had often to go outside into the lashing rain to the pigsty. I was feverish. I was sore. I slept and sweated or lay awake, cold as a corpse. Fear came upon me, and my heart lay heavier than the sands of the sea.

There are things we remember for no necessary reason and things we similarly forget, or seem to forget, conveniently or otherwise. Whether we truly forget anything or only misplace the clues to recollection is a question for philosophers and psychologists to ponder. But still I cannot bring to mind how it was I reached the pier and boarded the *Naomh Eanna*. I made no record of it and, scratch my head as I may, I cannot recall leaving home or crossing the bar of Aran, or any moment of that sorrowful departure, although the elements are few and their possible permutations limited enough to permit of easy invention. I remember only fragments of the voyage (much of it spent 'below'): the curraghs coming out from Inishmaan to take ashore returning islanders, and mailbags; and the enormous gloom, for the heavens were opened (though I saw no visions of God); and the waters beaded with rain, as reluctantly I entered a new captivity. The gloom and the rain seemed ponderously unnatural. It rained and never stopped, out of a still black sky.

We ground on, I remember, as if the voyage too would never stop, on to Inishere. Sandswept and desolate in the dark light it lay, and the curraghs darted through the rain over the oil-black millpond. It cut you to think that people lived out there and depended in this way for their survival. I forget if there were any to go ashore but remember being from that point on alone on the ship as she turned for home, except for a man from New Zealand and his son, who had come out for the trip. 'At least,' I managed to say, across the saloon, for we sat at opposite ends, 'the sea is calm.'

I had not shaved since reaching Aran, and must have cut a somewhat queer figure huddled in my trench-length oilskin. My rusty stubble had thickened only slowly, so that I seemed more unshaven than bearded, and thereby less than respectable. I told the New Zealanders my story as summarily as I could. I didn't really want to talk to them, nor they to me. Tell someone you are ill and on your way to hospital and they'll look at you oddly anyway, with a kind of uneasy suspicion, as if what you have might be contagious, as if death has put its finger on you, especially if you seem at all unwholesome, a head case, or somehow otherwise unaccommodated. So, understandably, the New Zealanders were not sure how to take me. But they soon preferred to leave me and went about the ship to watch the rain lash down upon the Burren and darken the dour headland which, even in fair weather, is known as Black Head. A crewman came in and talked to me a while, joking about the rain.

'I wonder is it raining on the moon?' he laughed, and at my incomprehension said did I not know there were men this moment going round the moon? 'Two hundred thousand miles from earth,' he said expansively, could I think of it? It was on the radio. 'And here we are,' he grinned, gesturing at what remained of the day outside, 'just twenty miles from Galway.'

I went out to take a little air myself. The deluge was so great it seemed to seal the world and you could think that you were on a voyage without destination or single plane of operation. You might, for example, sail straight across County Clare, or, right up into orbit to circumnavigate the moon. Still feverish and miserable, I felt as if I was in orbit, going round and round, remote from things, travelling into space, and somehow thought it to be pointedly poignant to be there, on Christmas Eve, dreaming of the tolling bell, cursing my luck, if not the day I was born.

6

*Christmas (Christmas!)*

'Religion?'

'None.'

The young woman, in her white uniform, exchanged a glance with her colleague, then looked superciliously across the counter at me, through the divided window.

'You must have a religion,' she said, resting her hands on the register, twiddling her biro.

'My religion is to have no religion,' I said as clearly as I could.

What kind of an answer was that? A new one on her, evidently. She wasn't pleased. She had other things to do.

'Protestant?' she asked impatiently. 'I have to enter a religion in the book. In case anything happens.'

'What?' I asked.

She frowned and then, finally, laughed.

'Why?' I continued, thinking I'd now got the upper hand, queer fellow as I must have seemed.

Her colleague giggled and turned away.

'I have no religion,' I insisted.

It was a matter of importance to me. But 'Protestant', she said, and wrote it down, and sent me on my way, too feeble to protest, with directions to the ward.

In those days, it seems to me, hospitals dwelt in a special kind of light, a kind of bleak fifties fluorescence, and an odour of stale flesh, subdued by the tang of sanitation. And now, I found, they dwelt in sanctity too. I was no expert on the subject but this one definitely seemed to me also to belong to another age. It belonged anyway to another world, as they all do, to no man's land, to limbo, to the world of thin partitions, fragility, tragedy and comedy, age and grief and deliverance, and every cliché you ever heard concerning our mortal condition, including the indomitable human spirit.

I slept brokenly that night but when I went, I sank submarine-deep, from the moment I got into my long shift and lay myself down. Questioning by nurses and doctors, to undergo prodding and probing (up my arse), to provide blood samples, to bare my poor lean rump and take a shot, and another shot, awoke me in a daze. They dragged me up. I looked into their earnest faces and sank back down. But I stirred too at hearing in the dead of night the coughs, splutters and ramblings of my fellow patients. Here were old men a-dying, some of them – old men complaining, joking, cursing, groaning, rambling, farting, snoring, old men with side rails round their beds to stop them falling out, or roaming.

I hadn't been in such terminally moribund society before, except once when I was a boy visiting my dying grandfather, who had cancer of the throat and could speak no more the bagpipe music that I used to love, whose favourite I knew I was. All he could do was creak and wheeze and gasp through his ruined chanter. Here were men like that on their last wind, forget their legs. Or had I in fact died en route and was now in a purgatory I'd never believed in, next step the operating theatre, and so on, out again to the island and back, and round and round for ever, in fair and foul weather? After my two months of solitary, I might be excused a bit of lunacy. Anyway, bedlam and babel reigned on the ward, especially with the likes of Loughrea's own uncontainable Pat Bourke there to wake even the dead, loud and vociferous, making his defiant nightly progress, bull-necked and pyjama'd, thrusting his arms into his dressing gown, rolling his burly way down the long ward bound for home, defying all comers in the politest terms. He was always keen to go home in the early hours of the morning, as who might not be, though first he had to call at such and such a place in Galway, Athenry or Ballinasloe where his sons were at a dance. It was always two in the morning and the cows hadn't been milked. Those boys would be the death of him, haring about the country.

Every night the ritual was the same. They said he'd taken a knock to the head. He had a fine head, a high – but now slightly puzzled – brow, and he held it up as he went, fixed on some private far horizon. During the day he'd calm down and talk quietly to the man next to him, telling him where he'd just been, reeling off names – Craughwell, Ballydavid, Portumna, Kilreekil, Kilchreest, Kilimor, Derrybrien, Gort, Aughrim … looking for his sons, buying a horse, selling sheep, seeing a man about a five-barred gate. He was never quiet for long. I expect the drugs he was on waxed and waned in their effects. Soon he'd be calling to the man across the way, shouting out to know the news, and if there wasn't any news, then 'a few lies' would do. Anything was better than nothing. He spoke, he seemed to think, for the benefit of us all, for the collective morale, despite the occasional despairing cry to the contrary. 'Och, shtap, shtap, won't you ever!' Then he'd maybe sleep but, once midnight came and went, up he'd stagger and away he'd be bound for Loughrea, the mere mention of which would bring derision to the lips of two or three who kept the long watch on the road to death and never seemed to catch more than a cat's nap. Loughrea to a Galwegian? Ask a Parisian what he thinks of Brussels. But they turned him about at the double doors, the two sallow-skinned night orderlies, one of them a gentle, coaxing man, the other a bit of a brute who enjoyed his strong-arm opportunity too much.

Beyond the doors, at who knows what ungodly hour, resounded another rude awakening, some rumpus with a tinker tribe cavorting in the corridor, trying to get one of them a bed for the night, a soft billet for the duration of the 'festivities', it was said. Was it for this they had a cattle grid, a first line of defence, at the entrance, or to keep us in? I remembered the taxi thuddering over it. But what hour was it now? I've no idea. A lost hollow hour before midnight or equally featureless space before dawn, disjoined and without end. One thing I remember feeling most was a miserable sense of failure, of a dream lost. Now there was no way I could truly say I'd spent a year on Aran when I was a wild young man, a wild colonial boy. Perhaps I'd never get back there? I lay envisaging the island and my house and pined for them and for the broken plot of the story I'd written for myself.

Imagine my hearth cold, and the rain running, like nature before the invention of the pitchfork, wild beneath my door. Imagine the wind soughing and blathering, the cymbal frantic at my doorknob, and the sea drawling and crashing and cascading on the rocks all the way from America. I imagined it, in fits and starts, but most of all I felt the rolling waves that took me down vertiginous depths of purest sleep into a morgue of stillness and repose. Was I exhausted? Was that what this was all about?

'Rise and shine!'

It's a false and cruel dawn indeed that calls the sick to muster, with mock cheer and banter, before even the hint of Christ's daylight has touched the sky. 'Rise and shine,' they called in self-parody, the swing-doors wagging wildly behind them, the lights flickering to blinding attention, trolleys laden, bed pans rattling, 'Rise and shine, boys! HAPPY CHRISTMAS!' I looked out from one eye across at the man next to me. Dead or alive? He didn't stir, jaw clenched in jaundiced sleep, a sleep like death, from which he roused at last as they returned and called again, and came by and said, 'Come along now, Joseph Prendergast,' as his mother might have done on a school day seventy or more years ago, pulling the covers from his clawed grasp, turning him, lifting him, bringing round the screen. For sure he'd need another note from mother today, asking to be excused games. I rolled over and peeped at my other neighbour, Tom the boy from Tuam, who'd chopped off his thumb under the edge of a refrigerator: Tom Thumb. He grinned and winked and gave me the thumb up.

I hauled myself onto my elbows and gazed around. Across the way another young man, from Sligo, with his leg in plaster suspended from a hook, waved at me, enquiring, 'You are the one from Aran off the boat?' I smiled and nodded and muttered inaudibly to him that I was. I realized his mistake. He was a lobsterman, he said; and he had a ruddy face like a cooked lobster, sanguine as a bowl of blood. He thought I was a fisherman, a trawlerman. I didn't disoblige him and it gave me special heroic status with him through my stay. I was into acting, it seems. He liked to wink hard and wave across at me and ask me how I was, me with my rusty stubble and wild eye, waving and winking back.

The able-bodied walking wounded among us made shift with our towels and washbags. Wisecracking and grumbling along to the wash area, catheter tubes in one hand, plastic bladders in the other, stiff-legged but game to the last, the codgers gathered, from all the wards together, and I a fly-by-night among them, waiting to brush my teeth. It was no good lamenting, I quickly saw. Here was the unforeseen, relationless, perfection of being, the thing itself, bare forked animal, boarding in death's border country, the common life, the poor people. What better? What had the world to offer that was more disencumbered, more real than this? Would I end up thanking my lucky stars to be there? I'll leave you to be the judge of that. All I know is that the exertions of the washroom put me to sleep. How long I slept I can't say but I woke not to the tinkling of a cymbal, as I might otherwise have done, but a small bell, heralding the priest on Christmas Day. I could see him from the corner of my eye coming down the row, blessing each patient, planting a wafer on one sleek or furry tongue after another, muttering a few words by way of blessing. As he came towards young Tom Thumb I shut my eyes and clamped my mouth. I heard him try to come to me and then a flurry and swish of his skirts and a nurse whispering something as she interposed herself between us in the little aisle beside the bed. What was it she whispered? Nil by mouth? Infidel? Anyway it was a moment of spiritual crisis allayed and he passed on about his master's work, leaving me to my fate, dealing out wafers as if there was no tomorrow. Who'd know if there were? So the day swam on, in and out of sleep, up and down the tide of noise that ebbed and flooded, as round followed round, as one was wheeled out to die, they said, and another wheeled in. Doctors and nurses came and went, asking questions, taking down stories.

'What happened?'

'I fell off a wall.'

'Where do you come from?'

'Clifden.'

'Did you pass any water?' asks the doctor now.

'D'you mean a bridge?' puzzles the grizzled old codger, eyes staring.

(The whole ward seems to have heard and erupts in laughter. Even the dead come briefly back to life, to laugh.)

'Did you eat at all? ...'

'Shtap, shtap!' protests another, at the prospect of an injection. 'Don't be telling me it doesn't hurt. I am me and I know.'

'Come on now, Michael,' two nurses circle the railed bed, one with hypodermic poised, and struggle with eighty-year-old flailing arms and kicking legs.

'No, you don't, look! ... I'm warning you. I'll break your faces if you come near me.'

'Oh, Michael ...' He wrestles with one of them, clinging on to her wrist with his bony hand, and the other darts in with her dart.

[ 117 ]

'Ach, you … bitches,' he subsides, defeated, drawing up his shift to look at the spot.

'Now you're not going to say that hurt.'

'Don't you tell me what hurts me.'

'It's for your own good, Michael.'

'You're poisoning me, damn you, the pair of you.'

'Nonsense.'

'It's for your own good. There now,' drawing the sheet over his scrawny flank.

'Good? Don't tell me. I am me and I know. I never had one in my life before and I was never on my back in bed like this.'

'Shtick, shtick,' the boys from Tuam are urging Tom Thumb, suddenly come of age by a digit.

'I am from Shpiddle,' a grizzled old terrier calls across to me out of the blue. 'I was in the Aran Islands myself fetching turfs in a hooker, forty years ago … All gone now … What age am I? Eighty-four. Eighty-five in the month of April. I will be going home in a week.'

Soon midday visitors rolled up, brazenly smuggling in bottles wrapped bottle-shape in crumpled brown paper, laughing and chattering, wishing happy Christmas to all and sundry.

I slept lightly after that and had a peculiar dream that I'd landed the *Naomh Eanna* on the moon. I thought I'd died and gone to heaven. But I was brought back down to earth with a bump, the rap of drum, the not-so-Elysian strain of accordion music rehearsing, and a general commotion as a combo installed itself at the head of the ward. Beds were shunted side on to make a bigger dance floor. A snare-drum rapped and rolled, and purred sedately, under the brush, a fiddle and a whistle played, and the accordion squeezed in and out, jigs and reels for doctors and nurses, priest and visitors, and walking wounded to surge up and down the widened aisle, with shrieks and whoops and cries of pleasure, as the dancers sped faster and faster, louder and louder, now and then careering into a bed, jolting awake its slumped corpse, on and on, over and over, round and round, the musicians upright, deadpan in a daze, their faces seeming the only immobile features in the room.

'Entertainment for the troops,' one nurse declared, renewing the rise-and-shine stand-by-your beds military metaphor of the hospital regime.

Another, halting by me, called wildly for 'Sir Roger de Coverley', the old English country dance tune. But Sir Roger de Coverley was nowhere to be found. Bottles went the rounds unwrapped. Hippocrates turned a blind eye. Symptoms took a back seat. The old terrier dog from Spiddal lit his pipe. The dancers danced. The drinkers drank. Then abruptly on the turn of a heel, the music halted, with one of those miraculously timed caesuras, and the band took itself off and most of its revellers with it to the next ward. The rest of us fell back wearied onto our matresses, as if ready for post-mortem's slab, to snooze or resume our vigil.

Whatever had ailed me (six of the soma and half a dozen of the psycho's my diagnosis now), I was a whole lot better the next day, a quieter day, the highlight of it for me provided by two freckled tinker boys who suddenly materialized beside my bed and began chanting rapidly, not quite in time together:

> The wran, the wran, the king of all birds
> St Stephen's day got caught in the furze

So up with the kettle and down with the pan
And give us a penny to bury the wran.

They paused while the bigger one proffered a little waxed
sweet box with a few coins in it, harps and hounds and hares to
chase in the wake of the wren. I turned and fumbled for some
change while they continued. I gave them what I had, more than
they expected, I saw, by the mid-verse look they shot at each
other:

Dreoilín, dreoilín, where's your nest?
It's in the tree that I love best.
In the tree, the holly tree,
Where all the boys do follow me.
So up with the kettle and down with the pan
And give us a penny to bury the wran.

Dara, a short bald man from Inishmaan, came in to find me,
asking to know was I the one from Aran? I was so, I said.

'I'm out of it these three weeks since,' he said, gently.

He had fallen after a wake and tapped his head. They brought
him across in the army helicopter from Casement Aerodrome.

'They did find me in the morning. Nothing I knew at all but
the next thing was, I was in this place.'

He paused and then asked, quizzically: 'You have been in
England?'

I had, I said, playing my cards close to my chest. I had. A few
months. As indeed was true. But on my saying my surname I
think he'd misheard, possibly MacNeelish or maybe 'Conneely',

a celebrated name on Inishmore. Why I should have wanted to masquerade I can only guess. Later the steward of the *Naomh Eanna*, in to see Dara, called by to say hello and know how I was, if not who I was.

Three of us then ended up that evening moved to a side ward down the corridor, myself, Tom Thumb, and P. J. O'Connor, a local publican and accordion player, a very big overblown man, grim-looking but genial at heart, an enormous acreage of pyjamas, in an agony with 'fluid in the legs'. He spoke through gritted teeth, but wouldn't be quiet. He'd had the ulcers fixed in October. 'The old barium meal, you know. Very tasty, I don't think.' Then it was a slipped disc, November – 'too much accordion' – and all manner of fierce stretching for a few weeks.

'I was only just off it Christmas week, and then the legs went. Fluid,' he declared.

See how he couldn't wear his trousers. See how his knees were swollen fit to burst. He drew the sheet aside.

'Even the least touch of that sheet's murder, you know, murder.'

P. J. was a man of influence. He knew everyone. He worked on the ward sister to get us a television and that's how we spent the next few days, talking about fluid and knees, discs and accordions, thumbs and fridges, Inishmore and finishmore, and watching movies: 'One-Eyed Jacks', and, in two parts, either side the 'Nuach', one specially chosen for me, 'The Old Man and the Sea' – call me Ernest.

After a week in there, seven days at ten shillings a day (I kept careful count), I grew restless and discharged myself, though there was no boat due to sail until the following Saturday (4 January). I found B&B at the Castle Hotel, the islanders' hotel, though it was as empty and silent as the grave that week.

It was a sign I was well again that I preferred to be out mooching round the town, killing time on foot, lurking here and there, rather than sitting cosy in hospital, for all that the sister, with evident pity in her look, tried to persuade me to stay. I was quite a sight now: some weeks unshaven, in full-length oilskin and my old cap (older than me, one my father had long ago discarded). There were places, like Lipton's tea rooms, that would not admit me, it amused me to discover. It's a strange experience, and one I'd prescribe for everyone, to be untouchable, for folk to back off at the mere sight of you. But I could catch up with my journal-keeping, sketching what I give you here, sitting in my hotel room, and I could look at the latest issue of the *Connacht Tribune*, for news of the wider western world, between excursions out along the shore down the bay, straining to see the islands, or round the harbour looking at the vessels there, feeling the tug on the heart's hauser, wishing to be away.

What news on the western Rialto? (Nurses offered nearly £2.10.0 per week extra to live on lonely Inishmaan, population 300. Galway County Council always has difficulty because nurses are reluctant to live on the islands, cut off from almost all the usual social activities of the mainland.) What news? (But things were even worse to the north at Inishturk, where despite an all-night vigil two curraghs were smashed and a quantity of turf for transport to the mainland washed away. There are seven houses on the island and thirty-five people, mostly bachelors, and eight school-going children. All the inhabitants are anxious to leave.) But it wasn't all bad in the western world. (Scientific knowledge has been piled on scientific knowledge. Man has orbited the moon and returned safely to earth. Fifty years ago the crossing of the Atlantic in a two-seater plane was man's greatest achievement. John Alcock and Arthur Whitten Browne landed one May morning in the bog at Derrygimla near Clifden, Co. Galway ...)

As for me, knowledge piled upon knowledge, I had my feet on the ground in my fashion, and set off when the day dawned for the harbour again, to board the *Naomh Eanna*. This voyage home was a slow one, the reverse of the route I'd come in on, though faster than it might have been, at this quiet time of year. You'll know by now all you need to know about the poignant, lyrical beauties of leaden and pewter light at scraich of day, of the sea silvered and shadowed, gulls mewling in the rigging as they glide and the crash of bow waves for accompaniment, the threshing out of the wake as the universal dimmer switch is opened up, making the lights inboard look jaded, like lights left on after a party, but somehow amplifying and enlivening the ceilidh music on the tannoy, as you chase home, in a chill wind, hanging on the rail, taking now a port, now a starboard watch, to see the Burren, to see the islands. I couldn't conceive of it ever being an unexhilarating experience for me, the most exquisite experience.

There was scarce a body aboard. Kate – the lady who'd suspected me of stealing her chickens – had made an early dash for the sales, if dash was the word in her case. She'd sat her great bulk in a corner of the saloon and drawn all her bundles round her, like a defence against the world's attentions. She acknowledged me just. Others there I didn't know, from Inishere, where we'd call first, and Inishmaan, our second port of call, or from the metropolis of Kilronan. I'd watched, as we wallowed and slurped, the

curragh slip back with its freight to Inishmaan, and then we powered up and headed for Kilronan. As we did so, a few people
came out to take the air and enjoy the view, to savour, as I
thought they must, the pleasure of completing their voyage home
to Ithaca. A bird-like woman in a scarf and belted navy gabardine
came out and stood by me.

'Are you on holiday?' I asked, for she had a little suitcase with
her.

'Pooh …' she started, 'holiday did you say? If it was holidays
I had I wouldn't be here, I'm telling you.'

'Is that so?'

'It is indeed,' she snapped, 'it is indeed.'

'It's a fine day,' I said, inanely.

'Ah, sure, the day's all right … It's a day, like any other. But
it's where you are and where you're going makes a day. I am going
to that place,' she nodded ahead, 'and I hate it more than any
place on earth. Thank God it won't be for long.'

I chuckled at her spleen. But she wasn't laughing. On she
went, with intensity.

'I never did like it even when I was a young girl. I couldn't get
out of it fast enough. I'm back now to sell my brother's place –
that's Seán Gill's, do you know, in Mainistir. He died last summer and I have been there since October, staying with the
brother-in-law.'

She'd got the wind behind her now.

'He's a comedian, forever persuading me to stay and keep
house for him. But believe me, when I've finished my business
I'm going back to civilization … to London.'

Had I the means, I might have bought her brother's house
from her, I felt tempted to say.

As I've said, I think the stigma of having been 'ill', of not being 'healthy', is one the world loves to batten on if it can. Your place in the scheme of things is altered. You're now rather less than the next man, for a time at least, and there's something people quite like about that. If you were a social challenge or any sort of threat to the daily order of familiar things, in any sense, you're less of one now. Men give you a wider berth when you're on the sicklist. Women, if they don't want to care for you, may look more askance than usual. You might not prove dependable, in your weakness. I sensed something of that Darwinian outlook, anyway, briefly on my return, a kind of embarrassment maybe.

Not that I wasn't welcomed back at the village as warmly as I could possibly have hoped to be. (I hadn't hoped at all.) I'd come back in relatively detached mode. But the idea of my 'illness' seemed to serve in my slow conversion from stranger to guest, which in the end would go further to find friendship. I had the predictable jokes about 'having had enough of the Aran Islands now surely' ('That's what I'd say, anyway,' said Stevie McDo-nough, like the lady on the boat a devotee of the 'gaol' school of thought, driving me home). But Mrs Feaney, Gregory and Mary were relieved to see me and to know I was all right. Of course it was an occasion. I had to have a tot of whiskey. Even old Mag-gie the crone came by to hear the crack. What had it been like? she wanted to know. She'd been in the same hospital herself, they told me. Which made her roll in her chair with laughter, like a child, so that the shawl fell back off her head, revealing a mass of grey and yellow-grey hair, an unruly stack, propped up by pins, and tied at the back with a black ribbon.

'And they did have men in with us,' she said, as we downed our drinks. 'Sure they did, men in with the women,' she shrieked and laughed and slapped her knees with her great work-thickened hands. 'Yes they did too. Kind of old men, you know, all bald. But there was cages round the beds, so they was stuck in, d'you see?'

'They must have been old women, sure, with no hair on their heads,' old Mrs Feaney reassured us, in an aside, tears of laughter in her eyes.

'Aye, there was men in it too,' Maggie carried on to herself, picking up her glass, 'sure 'twas great. And was there any women in with you?' she teased and flirted, all but toothlessly. 'There would have been, I daresay.'

'Oh,' I said, 'it was all women, you know. Except for me. I was the only man.'

'Ah, begob, the tongue on him!' she shrilled off into another fit of laughter.

And that was how I was welcomed home. But it had now grown late. The sky was turning blacker, from both a change in the weather and the approach of night. Maggie went off home. A Land-Rover (it must have been from Kilronan) came up the hill from the bay.

'I wonder is it the post?' asked Mary softly, almost to herself, as she cleared the glasses from the table and put the bottle in the cupboard.

That night I sat by my fire and read my mail. It was a Christmas bumper pile, including two cheques from magazines to which I'd sent articles on Aran, several weeks back, pieces about fishing. So I had a bonus I hadn't really expected, one of them for $165.00. A good friend from my Liverpool days and by then on Fleet Street sent me a copy of *The Third Policeman* by Flann

O'Brien (I don't think O'Brien's classic *The Poor Mouth*, so much more appropriate to my circumstances, had been reissued by then). But what intrigued me most in the post was a little book-let, a catalogue, that had got delivered, belatedly, among my things by mistake, as I supposed, selling Christmas cards, devo-tional objects (rosaries, crucifixes, 50-hour candles, Sick Call sets), etc. It wouldn't have been a surprise me to find it post-marked Rome, and dated the Middle Ages. But its sales language – the language of the sell as opposed to the cell – fascinated me and made me laugh aloud. It was of a kind you'd be hard put to invent, unless you were Flann O'Brien. Judging from the three sides of close copy in my journal, it went like this:

'There are really only three reasons why you should buy your Christmas cards from us. One reason is because they are exquis-ite. Another is because they are great value. The third is that you'll be helping the Missions. If these reasons do not appeal to you, fair enough. But we believe the radiant splendour and deli-cacy of these cards from various Irish firms will bewitch you. Their price and quality will magnetize you. ...'

Then there were 'Medals':

'The St Martin Medal, the St Martin you know and love, with the cat, dog and mouse in the background, all feeding from the same dish. These medals will enchant you with their elegance and delight you with their splendour. Even if you don't wish for the gold medals, the sterling silver ones are something to dream about. Five shillings the carat ...'

And candles:

'The St Martin Christmas Candle burns for 50 hours and we have never received a complaint about it in the eleven years since it appeared. Last year we sold more than ever and everybody loved it. No wonder. The usual Christmas candle is nice, the St Martin Christmas candle is majestic. Why not get one for your friends? They'll be in the seventh heaven with delight and will be enraptured with your choice. It costs only eight shillings. In short, it is perfection.'

And rosaries:

'Have you ever seen a Black Diamond? Well, the beads in this rosary sparkle and dance with the fire of black diamonds. On the continent they cost 25/– some years ago, but manufactured in Ireland and in a special box we still sell them at 15/–. We have rosaries in cut-glass crystal, or mother of pearl, the hallmark of quality. We have a world-quality bead for men on silver wiring, with pater beads capped and a glorious crucifix. Or a Connemara Marble Rosary made of the age-old marble. These will last for ever, particularly if kept in a rosary purse. Almost as old is the wood that is found in the bogs of Ireland. A Bog Wood Rosary costs 25/– and the wood from which they are made is calculated at being 8,000 years old. If your friend is fond of antiques, where will he get anything older, and for only 25/–? Or we have the Exile's Rosary. These are made of green durable material and the shamrock is stamped on every bead. With a Celtic cross attached they're a lovely gift for an exile at 10/6.'

I pondered the idea of the islanders studying these catalogues and putting in their orders. Later on in the year, out in the summer, a tinker came to my door, a three-day-stubble pedlar man, as wild in the eye as if he'd just stepped out of the eighteenth century. I'd seen his like in engravings. He had a very big cardboard box on his back, in a harness of postal twine. The box was by now only a quarter full of pegs and dishcloths and novelties. He came round to the back door where I was working in the August sun, untangling some fishing line. By this stage in my sojourn a character like this wasn't going to know me from a native and that's how I liked to play it. He set the box down and dipped in, to produce one item after another for my delight: a nativity scene in a globe, which he shook to make it snow and patiently showed me how the flakes fell; a wooden spoon; and so on; but I wanted nothing. (I wondered if he might have a world-quality bead in there for men on silver wiring?) At last, in desperation he came up with a metal tea-strainer, the kind of thing you put over your cup to catch the leaves, a very plain little sieve.

'Here, sir,' he said, as if writing copy for St Martin, twiddling it round under my nose, 'all gilded and silver-dashed.'

Worth all the tea in China, I thought. Each cup poured through this strainer would be better than the one before, the purest nectar. How could I resist? And off he went with my florin, round the houses, on to the next village. What kind of a world was it still? How poor the poor in the western world?

We had a very cold snap, numbingly cold, for a few days, and there was nothing much to do but burn fuel and go out on the road meanwhile, to warm the soles of your feet as if they were the cockles of your heart, for exercise and diversion, notably now to spot for geese. Geese had flocked in great numbers into the west at the year's turn, with the cold and wild weather, and the prospect of seeing and hearing them rise from Oghil Lough was more than worth the bitter cold. Folk remarked on them, they were such a phenomenon. (Though not one did I see.) Then we had greenhouse weather. But Gregory assured me cold days lay ahead, make no mistake, and I decided, with my cheques to put in the bank and an unaccounted surplus to spend, I'd go to Galway to attend to some business. I had already broken the pledge I'd made to myself not to set foot on the mainland for a year. Besides, I now saw, voyaging to and from Galway was integral to island life.

Until I began to examine my journal and letters and to write this up, I had always in my mind conflated my return from hospital with the return leg of this subsequent journey. It improved a good tale in the telling. And that's how we prefer things, as you know. Autobiography, oral or written, is everyman's genre, the impoverished genre of the people, the genre of the poor (of means as well as wit?), the democratic genre. That's what makes it the worthiest of them all. Who's not got a story to tell? Who won't be silenced? (Every bore on earth.) But no wonder the autobiographer tries so persistently to compensate for his plight, his imaginative poverty, his inability to figure other worlds of mind and soul from the template of his own, consciously or unconsciously, straining at the leash of fact and haring off, unruly, unskilled, and even remorsefully, into the true fresh woods and pastures new of fiction. Or so at moments of reflection (enemy of promise) he might think or fret. As if our memories are any more than tea-strainers, gilded and silver-dashed in the mind's eye. As if it isn't all made up, and skill or the lack of it the issue.

My journal makes it absolutely clear. On Wednesday 15 January, at 3.30 p.m., I sailed from Kilronan to Galway, to start a new regime regarding provisions, to order bacon and other supplies direct from Galway, once a fortnight, for two or three months, from Naughton's; to have some peat delivered, for the poetic flavour of the smoke and quality of embers; to order a pair of heavy island-style tweed trousers, slapstick trousers they turned out to be, from Padraig O'Maille, for £5 (they chafed so much they proved unwearable; I used them to patch my old ones); and to buy in new tackle for the coming months' attempts at fishing. I sailed in with Mrs Feaney and it was dark when we got ashore, a blustery night with gobs of rain on the wind. Mrs Feaney went off to stay with friends. I went back to the Castle and on Thursday pursued my usual course in alienation studies, mooching round the town, haunting the docks, where boats and cargo vessels, like *La Roche* from Bordeaux, were moored and mooring, and thinking, as one of the seamen called down 'C'est bien ça' to the Irishmen ashore, how next, maybe, after Aran, I should go to sea, seriously give up everything and go to sea. Like the archetypal stranger, I recognized no homeland and, though I had friends and family, I had a cold streak in my heart that made me care for no one and nothing but the possessionless possession of the voyage. Or so I thought, guided by the kind of things I'd read.

I set off for home (how natural that 'home' began to be: I was more at home and less) at 7.30 on the Saturday morning for the eight o'clock sailing. At the harbour that morning wind scudded among long puddles and the rain made the lamps at the roadside and on the various vessels bleary-eyed. There was a real thickness to the dark. It was like walking into the bottom of a sack. One or two taxis and vans swished heavily to the end of the jetty. A great corrugated iron dome nearby, housing some kind of processing plant, rattled and banged, creaked and groaned on the wind, the way a dutch barn will out on a hill farm, geese clanking in the yard, gloomy oak trees rocking round the steading. I had tons of stuff in a couple of unwieldy sacks and struggled along, joined as

I went and passed by little groups or individuals absorbed in their own struggles, wading through the glistening dark, out of the streets of the town. They were nearly all women, heavily laden with stuff from the sales.

By the time I got aboard, the saloon was already quite packed about with rolls of carpet and lino, broom handles, boxes of china, and so on, stuff sent down the previous day. Many of the women went below to sleep. Others – all of them arriving now, in ones and twos, their hands full – chatted and turned, clearing spaces, like poultry pecking and clucking away: the womenfolk from every tribe and faction on the islands. There was old Mrs Feaney, buttoned up, headscarved, half hidden by her bundles. Apart from the women and myself, there were a few old men, a Guard returning to Kilronan after a spot of leave, and a nurse, bound for Inishmaan. The concern of all was would we sail at all, would we be home that day? After three days' excitement ashore, out of their element, the women were all impatient to have the sea about the island and their four walls around them and the joy of their goods to unpack. There was some worrying delay. The weather forecast promised a gale eight, rising to severe gale nine, and the first signs of it were lunging in the rigging and spluttering about the town.

We sat stoically, with the boat creaking and heaving against the timbers of the pier. The radio came on as we waited for the jury to return and pronounce its verdict, playing regular jigs and reels, and already the *Naomh Eanna* jigged and reeled and beat her foot at the wallowing quayside, as if drunk, and the day scarcely dawned. The Guard went out to be sick, poor man, and we hadn't gone a yard. Then word went round that we'd cast off.

We were edging out into the bay. Everyone visible was visibly pleased, as at last we pitched up, and crashed down, and wallowed, and rose and crashed. The old men, *omertà* in their hearts, packed down their pipes and smoked, elbows on their knees, and stared at the floor, as if this were merely a short bus-ride upon a steady road. The tannoy blared. We were due in Kilronan at two-thirty, such a long time because we were going round the islands. I seemed to adjust to the boat's motion without ill effect, and, because it was such a dramatic morning, I went on deck to watch the storm. Great black waves with tall and very white breakers raced towards us. It was the most dramatic sight, with a delayed dawn breaking over the hills of County Clare and sea birds grabbed by the wind and taken away past us at breakneck speed. (Downrail the Guard spewed and spewed what by now could only have been thin air.)

They took a very dim view of it indeed when the captain announced, an hour out, that we must turn back. He had no choice. It was too bad and getting worse. They couldn't cross.

'Of course they could,' said Mrs Feaney, 'sure, they're no good.'

It was 'cutting off Kilronan for the sake of the islands', people were saying, in the usual way, as if Inishmore was a continent half the size of America. It wasn't crossing the bar of Aran was the problem, as the crew maintained, but standing off the islands for the curraghs.

The women who'd gone below, whether they slept or not, had no way of knowing whether they were coming or going. So when they were summoned up as we stood moored again at Galway pier, some of the more sleepy-eyed thought for a moment they were home. But when the word got round, the more belligerent of them exploded. They demanded to see the captain. They called his manhood into question. They railed and mocked and jeered, scolding like fishwives, stranded with their shopping on Galway pier. There was much hectic rummaging to find joints of meat, sausages and rashers, to get them to a fridge. (I stored my meat in the ship's fridge, after some whispering with the steward.) We would sail on Monday, 9 a.m.

I'd had enough by now of Galway, reading in the hotel, or flâneuring round the town. Sunday was a day of perfect, pristine sunlit aftermath; out along the bay you could see the islands, thirty miles away, so clearly you felt you might be there in a stride. A lot of the women, old Mrs Feaney among them, had got wind of P.J. Mullen's trawler at Rossaveal and taken taxis out there. They were already at home when I landed, to be greeted by Gregory, busy in a commotion on the quay, arms flailing, stick waving, as skidding and complaining cattle were manhandled into the sling and lowered, bellowing to the bleak sky, into the hold. Gregory had just sold some stock to a Galway jobber. (Bullocks on the hoof were going in Galway market for between £8.10s and £9.5s the hundredweight, and heifers £8.5s and £8.15s; and even with the jobber's commission taken off, he'd done well. So he told me. It was great money.) A belated insert in my journal, prompting me to remember an unusual scene, impossible to forget, seems to show that this was the day the children returned to school on the mainland. Anyway, as the *Naomh Eanna* crossed the bar, the girls – one leaden morning of farewell and tears – all gathered in the stern, shrieked in a single orchestrated keening, so shrill and clear it stopped the day (to dwell upon exile, past and future, or hope lost, and boats missed). It was the most dramatic thing, resounding away up through Kilronan to the hill above.

We got my sacks and Mrs Feaney's bundles into the back of Stevie McDonough's pickup and ran off home for another home-coming, a fry-up, more whiskey, and an excited unpacking, the high point of the year. Brooms and other larger items – carpets and rugs, lino – apart, Mrs Feaney had three very big cardboard boxes of excitement to reveal to Mary: plates and cups, cornflakes (she laughed), tins of paint, wallpaper, turpentine, towels and sheets, pillows and napkins. Each item was taken out and unwrapped, unfolded, examined, shown to Mary. Advice as to quality was sought from both Mary and myself. There, she had one-and-six off these plates and tenpence off those and that was twenty-five shillings but she got it for seventeen-and-six. What did you think of it? (Have another drop. Mary, pour the man another drop to drink. Mary huffed, turning from the frying pan.) She liked the stair-carpet very much and it was rolled out across the floor. They had some with blue in and one with a light colour but she preferred the red patterned and it wouldn't show the dirt. The scatter rugs were not very satisfactory. They looked as if you might have made them yourself. Here, now, look at this – a bit of frivolity – a plastic coal bucket. It'd be good enough if you kept it from the fire and didn't rest the iron in it, observed Mary, managing in her inimitable way to find something deflat-ing to say about most of the purchases. She sat now by the stove with a light teacup in her hand, plucking the rim between finger and forefinger, indicating without a word but a look of disap-proval that it wouldn't be long in being broken.

'Sure we do break a lot in the summer,' said Mrs Feaney, look-ing at me, opening another box of dishes with unalloyed enthusiasm, as if the whole business were a preparation for the summer sport of crockery breaking. Then I had to look at this. Two rolls for only seven-and-six, the last two they had. And these two and here a bit of border for three-and-nine the yard, but it's good and deep. Could I hang wallpaper? We'll do a little hanging later on and some light painting.

'Ice-blue,' said Mary, holding up a tin of paint, with a shiver of disapproval, before going off to the scullery.

'Well, that's the lot,' said Mrs Feaney, sitting back triumphantly, among the litter of boxes and entrails of newspaper packing, 'and what a lot there is.'

And so I imagined all the womenfolk who had been aboard, at that moment, up and down the island, regarding their spoils, in January, the women's month for conspicuous pleasure and consumption, their heart's delight to hit the waves for grey Galway's rock-bottom sales, their hearts raised on return, to unwrap new crockery, bed-linen, carpets, oilcloth, cutlery – with winter yet to come, in frosty February, with biting cold from dawn to dusk, and storm and fog, and sinking gloom of submarine shadow (crustacean consciousness, unmentionable sexuality), time to endure. As to the menfolk:

*We had no milk today until gone nightfall. [I scribbled over the fire that night, porridge piping.] Gregory only got back from selling his cattle at 7.30. 'He's a drap taken,' said old Mrs Feaney indulgently, 'he's only now come in and gone out again to milk the cow just the same, poor man. Mary's in a fit!' When he came back he was in a high state, joking about women's work, how he could make cakes, and how there was no money in the land, and how he'd got a bloody soaking on*

*the way to Kilronan that morning. On my nocturnal rabbit netting*
*trips I've started to go up to Dun Aengus. Gregory said to take care,*
*there are big crevices where you could break your leg. Mrs Feaney said*
*there are fairies. (The second time I've heard her say so – now* AD
*1969.) At this Gregory changed his attitude and said – in a phrase he*
*seems to like – ah, sure, the night is like a day on account of the moon.*

# 7

## *Saints and Sinners*

In the minds of the devout, I was Inishmore's sinner in residence that year. There I was, as clear as day, a man never christened, for one thing (I never concealed the fact when the topic of religion arose; it was a provocation to me); and a man … a fool married or not married? Though I can never bring myself to begin to believe in any of the metaphysics (is evil metaphysical? how on earth could it be?), I have as good a sense of right and wrong as the next man. Not that I would say as much for my judgement at all phases of the moon. Few things resemble the moon more than what? A head of Guinness looked full in the face. It splits my head now to recall those passages in my adventure that were scribbled in the ink of Guinness or reborn in the ashes of Phoenix lager.

One night at Dirrane's I disgraced myself in a lunatic fashion. Do not ask me precisely what I did or said but I made myself non grata, not with Dirrane I think, though he was as soberly inscrutable as ever, but with the clientele. There was a tourist there, like a migrant bird blown off course, right out of season, and I spoke to him. He was a young Englishman, an exotic, with a double-barrelled name that sounded very like Word-Perfect and that, in my cups, is what I began to call him, Mr Word-Perfect – this in the days before the software. It was a soft thing to do. To their great credit, the fellows in the pub didn't like it, my upstart presumption with their guest. But I did worse. I said something against the Irish language. No one respects the ancient languages more than I do, as cultural wonders and treasure troves and inspirations in all their teleologies, revelations and reproaches for all we think we know and believe we've put behind us. No one mourns the inaccessibility of them more than I, slow at learning as I am, a middling scholar only.

The thing at Dirrane's was begun with a quip, about something I'd heard an old man say in hospital, how people in Clifden took a dim view of official forms in Irish.

'Might as well be in French,' he said, and it seemed to me that if that's what he thought, well, he'd every right to think it, and every right to say it. He was Irish. He lived in Ireland. But for me to question the universal inviolable value of the Irish language, insofar as I did, on the Aran Islands, in Dirrane's pub – it was as reckless as blaspheming Allah in Mecca. It was the closest of calls that the bachelors didn't work me over that night. It was stir-crazy season for them, just at the outer edge of winter, on the long boundary with spring. They certainly debated it, out in the lane, for I was among them and could pick out the weight of deliberations. What held them off was old Mrs Feaney getting to know of it. They decided – which was not a whole lot better for me, but better – to smoulder on, to hold it against me, pending who knows what processes, what avenging politics, in the Guinness courts? I could expect a clattering some black night out on the road, I knew. The schoolmaster advised me so as he and I (both tenants of the Feaneys) redecorated Mrs Feaney's bedroom.

'Rough justice', he called it, with a raised eyebrow and a smile. 'Or you'll get a rock through your window for a warning.'

(He'd once lined a cupboard, he said, and so took the lead in our effort, not a right angle to be found anywhere, or a smooth surface from floor to ceiling.)

At least I had the wit in the stark light of day to steer clear for a while of those avenging Marcuses and Daras. Gregory at once knew all about it – as who did not? small news speaks volumes in the wilderness – and he had no time for it (nor it seemed did my self-appointed enemy Colm). It was one chance day, not long after the night of the hard words, that I met with Gregory on the road and we got to know each other a little better, over and above the very spare context of the day-to-day, 'Fine evening', 'Fine evening', 'I see you have your street swept', 'It is windy' class of exchanges. There wasn't much to it but it was a step in the right direction. As it happened, it provided me with a startling revelation of some of the strange wonders that could go on in the language I'd been so unjustly judged to have maligned. I was walking east on the metalled road, just beginning the hill up to Oatquarter that morning, a bright airy day with a cold edge to it. The past few days had been perishing.*

*On 17 February I noted: 'Snow and frost. Across in Connemara the country like a glacier out to the 12 pins. The sea strange in its mobility beside the frozen coast. Out cutting briars on the rocks my knuckles turned as raw and

That day the dunes shimmered in the breeze and the sea in the bay, with the wind behind it, ran with a thrilling rip into the shingle and sand, spluttering weed ashore, booming up and rattling back, pounding again, scattering a flock of waders that swirled round to realight, like sparks struck up by the hammering sea. You'd have been happy leaning there against the wall all day, under the dunes, in the breathtaking ozone air, watching the gulls, listening to the sea and the piping shorebirds, shielding your eyes from the wintry glare, or levitating among the grasses on the dune, dreaming your dream, were it not so cuttingly cold.

I took it into my head, suddenly, that while the wind was in the east I'd try to get down to the Atlantic shore, along the rocks and among the pools towards Blind Sound. I'd seen some spars down there, big bevelled spars that would burn like tinder, if I

---

as cold as the knuckled limestone itself, numb and aching and grazed, as I reached in the clefts where the brittle briars run, up round Dun Aengus, in the chevaux de frise (stonework defences) – should be chevaux de freeze. Briars for the fire, by the crooked yard. Frost flames. As promised we've had frosts this month that've stayed all day. The island rings like metal, shod hoof on stone, a bell, like glass, clanging in the hard east wind; night as cold as the stars, the island a star in its cold sea firmament. Or, about-face, it sinks eerily, muffled in fog, like a submarine listening for the enemy, dank, as it is now, while I write.'

And on 23 February: 'We've had no boat for ten days now, no water in the tap either. Everything still frozen. But if someone called round tonight they'd find warm welcome here. I found a prop and sawed it into logs today, a resinous, tough piece of wood. Burns with a scent and occasional snap like a firecracker. It's very soothing to sit and watch the wood disintegrate slowly until it stands upon nothing, like a web in the grate, with strong blue and yellow flames floating across it, not enough to thaw the stars, just enough to cook my shins, to defy the east wind a moment. Driftwood usually burns with rainbow colours, with shimmering cockerel hackles, but mostly if it's really salt-dry it flares up and vanishes in an instant, as suddenly as a bunch of hay.'

could bear them home, and some old resinous props, 'pit props' I always called them. So I pushed my back up off the wall and headed for Gort na gCapall boreen. Then Gregory came rattling down, driving the Big Fella between the shafts of a flat cart, on an errand to Kilronan. He reined the Fella in and, as the temperamental beast backed and faltered, offered me a ride. As I was keener to get to know Gregory than to gather spars (even if the next tide might bear them off, unless they were really jammed), I thanked him, and hitched myself up on the heels of my hands onto the cart as the Fella arched his neck and sidled, dangling my legs tinker-style on the near side of the horse's rump. It was a great moment for me, in the depression that clouded my heart after the Dirranean debacle. We chatted along, neither of us quite at ease.

'You'll not be learning any Irish,' he declared pointedly, raising his voice above the hooves and grinding wheel rims, 'if you don't mix with the people. But you are like myself, I'd say, one for your own company.'

I said I knew what he meant and so we went on, more or less silently, touching on the 'missus' briefly. How funny it was I didn't seem to miss her too much, he observed, pointedly, making me feel doubly uncomfortable. She must have been troubled over Christmas? I could see him listening to the tenor of my answers as much as to the answers themselves, testing me, observant, canny, tickled at heart; and then letting go of it, not to be ill-mannered. We wound up the hill, and came round to the hairpin by the smithy. The smith was out of doors working with a rasp at the toe of a brown mare. A couple of men, caps down over their brows, leant by and watched. The Big Fella flattened his ears as we

approached and Gregory muttered a few calming words. Hardly
bothering to look up, one of the men called out sharply in a
stream of Irish that to my ears did not sound much like a common greeting. In fact it sounded abrasive and, I thought, hostile.
Gregory responded in similar vein. The man called after us again,
and Gregory once more replied, without turning – and so on, to
and fro, as the horse climbed on and we slipped from hearing. My
curiosity as to the meaning of these civilities or incivilities upon
the road got the better of me. I asked to know what the man had
said. I thought perhaps he was hurling insults at my head. But it
was a kind of saintly flyting, a game.

'He gave me St Enna, St Benedict and St Giban,' Gregory
explained (I derive the names from a later conversation). 'Then I
gave him St Fursey, St Conall and St Brendan of Birr. Then he
gave me St Berchen, which was right, being the fourth of the
three I gave him, and he gave me St Kiernan and St MacLongius
too. Then I was giving him St Cathrodhochus, St Assurnaidhe
and St Brecin when we came away.'

'You know a lot of saints' was all I could think to say, in my
amazement.

'I know six score anyway,' said Gregory with an odd mix in his
voice of defiance and mockery, 'I can give as good as I get in that
line.'

He turned to speak to his horse and I to wondering how there
were not only more things in heaven and earth, as I knew, but far
more saints, than were dreamt of in my philosophy. The heavens
and the earth and the serpent sea in such stark combination as
you find upon the islands must concentrate the mind upon sanctity and virtue. Which I suppose is metaphysical? At any rate, it's

well known that you'll find as many saints in the history of Aran as there are angels on the head of a pin. Their legacy is every-where, especially in plaster, but in itself not enough to sustain life for even the most religious island soul, let alone a secular dreamer like me. More to the point for me was the tantalizing glimpse I'd had into a world of verbal playing, of local familiarity, of a resilient, combative out-of-doors culture deeply involved in the texture of language itself, and the sharp rhythms of this particu-lar kind of call and response. In other instances, I later learned from Colm, time still whiled itself away in punning games, seiz-ing upon the multiple meanings and shades of meaning in Irish words, where the object was to leave your opponent stuck for words. By turns quick-witted and tedious, he seemed to imply.

Now the days began to lengthen. Ravens courted along the cliffs. The last goose cloud stood high on frosty air. Hearts rose up and would not be put back. One day the sun shone; the next was a day of rain and wind. The wind moaned and groaned at being shut out everywhere. Thatches got dishevelled. Your view through the window was so distorted by the rain the village houses seemed to sway in the wind. Their chimney stacks seemed to bend over to hold their roofs on. Men flashed by in one direc-tion sailing on bicycles down the lanes, off to milk, silver cans clattering. And they came wading back, taking big swinging strides at the pedals, wobbling with the peaks of their caps and their noses nearly touching the front wheel, as if scenting their way home rather than look the wind and rain in the eye.

I had a visitor, a former colleague by then working in Fleet Street, came out with beefsteaks and oranges, for three days between sailings. I had not been overjoyed to hear he was coming – anything unanticipated jolted my story-line – but I enjoyed the company when the time arrived, even if it tore me from my world and intensified my sense of alienation. I met him off the steamer, a queer hawk he looked, in his camelhair coat and black city shoes, with his rolled umbrella and suitcase, as he came ashore. We'd been conspirators and traitors together. We'd formed an escape committee, to ship out from Liverpool for national jobs in London, to escape the parochial. But what had we in common now?

It was grey and cold during his stay. I took him beachcombing and we found a seven-foot spar on the landward shore, a beauty, with a neck, like the neck of a vase, at one end, and a taper, all worn smooth by the sea, at the other. It was at least a foot wide at its widest and about two and half inches thick. And it was resinous. It sprang under the rocks I struggled to crack it with, and batted them back at my feet and shins. My visitor, I realized, felt alarmed at the wild violence I brought to bear upon that spar of wood. But he didn't know as I did the true material value of it, its scarcity, its firepower. It was a long way from a day's work in Fleet Street, where he would soon be reinstalled. A liberal man at heart those days, he'd had no choice but to serve his time on the society diary of a Tory rag, the job he could get, to make his escape into the great world. He left me a copy of the paper he worked on.

'Not something I'd sully my arse with; all that smudgy lead,' I wrote in my journal.

Despite the upset at the pub, I was more at home, and less, as the days drew out inchmeal to seedtime. (By 12 March I noted there was daylight at 8 p.m.) But still the sea bucked and kicked in its winter coat and wouldn't take a rider readily, or nurse my nightlines. The islandmen were on the shore to gather weed, or in the fields, digging and talking as they worked. Above the blowing Atlantic talk's free and time by the mile runs, as far as eye can see: many missed boats to America, many losses and denials, and dearth of women.

'Somebody has to stay,' says Michael. 'That's how it is here now, that kind of way,' turning his back to dig, thinking of his sons.

He'd grown uneasy with me again, all at once, for a week or two, after I'd come upon him by the graveyard below Kilmurvey, one sharp evening at twilight, above the bay. You could hear the sea tolling, running high, sifting the sands of time. The tides were big, as the moon reached its full yawn. (The sound of the sea was always audible. If only the typesetter could provide a side-gloss and notation for all its registers, crescendi, decrescendi, fortissimo, allegro, con brio, pianissimo, pipistrello, never lost and out of hearing, somewhere at the bottom of a conch at low spring tide, or cannonading 1812, storming the cliffs at high.) Michael leant on the wall by the road, elbows raised to shoulder height, hands linked (nose, mouth and chin pressed against them) and, gazing at the unequal ranks of tombs and graves, crosses and headstones, raised his head a little to tell me glumly where his grave was waiting for him.

'Full of old bones and dust. My family. All my family's bones and dust in it, briars and thistles.'

I told him how an early visitor to the island, very long ago, another man from Wales like myself, had put it about that human corpses on Aran did not decay. Giraldus or Gerald, as his name was, claimed that on Aran you could go and see all your ancestors whenever you liked and find them looking as fit and healthy as yourself. I don't think he appreciated it.

But before he knew it the lazy beds would be sprouting haulms. There'd be blight on the damp June air, calling for 'burgundy mixture', calling up the starving shades of hunger. There'd be pilgrims landing at Kilronan. Jarveytime would be here again and strangers to chat up and charm, fares to charge; sweaters and bonnets to be sold, in creamy white or dyed in not-so-fast indigo: the womenfolk's winter's knitting to dispose of – cable, diamond, trellis, net, carrageen moss, honeycomb, fern, figure-of-eight, zigzag, trinity, tree-of-life, ladder, crooked road, marriage lines, bobaleen, castle, anchor – old designer riddles in thick wool, unwritten, known by heart, unique to the household. The women knitted their wintering souls together, against the hour, against the weather, as once they'd knitted in the open fields, singing together. And thinking ahead myself, to the days when the sea would come to hand, and you could walk along with it, like a horse broken to the rein, with less risk of being swept away, I made enquiries and, as I scribbled it in my journal, set off to buy a pair of pampooties:

*The pampootie, as readers of Synge will know, is a kind of moccasin of uncured cowhide, traditionally worn (with the cowhair on the outside) by the islanders and valued for the adhesion and purchase it affords upon wet rocks. It is also ideal wear aboard a curragh, because it is so light, and should you fall into the sea you can swim in it more easily than in a boot, not that you will swim for long. Few on the big island wear them any longer now in 1969; they're not exactly winter wear either, and I think you will soon come to see why. Nonetheless I thought I'd like to have a pair to try upon the rocks as the season's fishing I dream of night and day approaches. The Feaney brothers assured me that if I would get pampooties anywhere I'd get them, all right, at Bungowla, and they told me where to call. And so I set out to walk the long and wild road to the far west of the western world. It soon began to rain as I went along, and then to pour torrentially, enough to all but take your breath away.*

*By the time I made the summit above Bungowla I was wet in every pore. The wind buffeted and blasted and snatched and pummelled and I could hardly see my way ahead for the rain. It was impossible to see across to Connemara, where yesterday the view had been crystalline. The road ran down to the village like a river and tumbled out beyond it in a rubble of boulders into the fleeting sound between the cape of Inishmore and the first of the two small outcrop islands, the Brannogues or Brannocks. Out beyond the sheltering rocks the Atlantic roared like the end of the world, all the way from America. Not a sign of life stirred in the village. It looked as grim and desolate as the slate-quarrying villages of Snowdonia, where mountains of shale loom above the narrow streets and it never stops raining from cradle to grave.*

*But there comes a point in a drenching when you progress from discomfort and vain efforts to keep your collar up, your sleeves down, your feet dry, into miserable abandon and then pleasure like a child stamping in the puddles, at least until you begin seriously to perish. It was in such happy spirits that I paused and saw a diminutive lone figure appear from the side of one of the cabins. He stood, apparently indifferent to the weather, away down below, and looked the long road up at me. A dog trailed out after him and now the two watched my progress down the hill towards them. In another world it might have been that I was expected. Here it was just that I promised diversion and perhaps custom too. The man, a tall grizzled man, one of those who wait until Sunday before shaving, called to greet me as I drew near and when I reached him I explained my business and he understood what I wanted and led me off the way he had come.*

*The back, leeward door stood open to make the best of the daylight and the rain ran and blew inside the house. It streamed across the floor as far as an island of sodden rags in the middle of its path and then oozed on and slipped out beneath the front door in a broad delta. A small flock of fowls that had seemingly been sitting quietly enough in a dingy corner were, as I came in, bullied in a commotion of arms and legs and clucking to the end of the room by another tall unshaven man. When he had done, he turned with a smile to greet me. One of the fowls flew up to the loft and with queer nervous jerks of its head eyed us beadily from the top of the ladder. The old beshawled woman of the house stood to greet me and almost at one and the same time railed at the fowl which was now peeping from deeper in the loft, clucking and burbling to itself. One of the old woman's feet was heavily bandaged and a clump of lifeless yellow-grey and frozen toes protruded from the bandaging. She hobbled about on her heel in great discomfort to sit me down, to pour me some tea from the range, where the pot stewed next to a mound of steaming potatoes. (Another scene from Van Gogh.)*

*The walls of the room were clean and bright, decorated with religious pictures and objects of devotion: pope and Kennedy, crucifixes, the vision of our lady at Knock, such as I had upon my own walls, or had seen on the mantelpiece at Kil-na-cer. (The sort of thing you might order up from St Martin, priceless items, each one a superior purchase.) The men sat by on a bench, and leaning forward, elbows on*

*knees, all ears and observation, left the old woman to do the talking.*
*She was animated by this diversion, on such a dismal evening of*
*wilderness and wet, and although I sometimes found it hard to com-*
*prehend her, we enjoyed a conversation, punctuated by snatches of*
*song, and extraordinary excitements. She was especially agitated when*
*I said I came from Wales and she sprang up, quite regardless of her*
*bandaged foot, and unhooked a calendar from the wall. It was the cal-*
*endar of a building firm, bearing a view of Milford Haven. She had*
*a son working there. His name was Michael Faherty. Would I know*
*him? A big man. He had not been home these six years. I explained*
*that I came from the north, and she checked herself palpably and set the*
*calendar aside, as if to show she saw through her enthusiasm as well as*
*I. She was for a moment subdued. Then she turned and invited me to*
*sing, and having no voice, and not the wit to know it didn't matter, I*
*declined. So she sang, some mournful nasal song in Irish. As we were*
*so engaged one of the men had slipped out and now returned and emp-*
*tied a bucket of wet pampooties on the floor. At first I thought they*
*must be a kind of cured fish. They certainly didn't resemble footwear.*
*They looked wet, and so they were, for that is how pampooties must be*
*kept. They are worn, however, not so much wet as damp, over thick*
*socks, because, being uncured, when they dry they dry as stiff as boards*
*and are unwearable until soaked again. As I sat puzzling at them,*
*trying in the gloom to make out what kind of fish they might be, a*
*third man and a woman in a shawl entered and sat down to enjoy the*
*party. The old lady came to the end of her song. Cups of tea were*
*poured and attention turned to what I now accepted were in fact the*
*pampooties that had been the object of my errand.*

*The man of the house, as I took him to be, stooped over them and*
*began to inspect them one by one. Another man from the village*

*appeared in the doorway and after a few casual words with the old woman came in and took a seat. There was quite a company gathered and as yet no conversation to hold it together. Everyone regarded the pampooties, as the man picked one after the other up by its cord and slapped it down again. He seemed to be grouping them according to size and sorting them into pairs. At last two pampooties in what was deemed my size were fished out and held against my foot. The old woman now took over. Her asking price was 14/–. Before I could say anything this prompted immediate comment, in Irish, from one of the spectators, and a sharp rejoinder from the old woman in return. I explained that I only had 10/– to spare at the most. (It's a lot of money as I live now.) Looks were exchanged. The man sifted, arranged and rearranged the sodden footwear once again. The spectators began to talk and nod among themselves. Something was going on but I couldn't tell just what. But I assumed the asking price was at issue. At last the outspoken man removed his pipe and made his point once more, again in Irish. Upon this the old woman rose, hobbled into the arena and picking up one of the selected pampooties forced it half onto her bandaged foot. She challenged all comers: the pampooties were strong and well made. She hopped about to continue her demonstration, the pampootie beginning to dangle. But the critic again removed his pipe and spoke once more words that displeased her.*

*'The gentleman wants to buy his pampooties,' she protested for my benefit, and then snapped out something in Irish.*

*The man stuck to his point and in the end I obtained my pampooties for 8/–, and I thought that was the end of it, a bargain if ever one was made. The people came out to see me off and I walked back, my pampooties under my arm. As I went the rain eased and the cloud began to break. By the time I reached Kil-na-cer, the stones were gleaming and the sky held frozen blue chasms beyond the cloud through which brief and icy sunlight shone ethereally. But I felt increasingly downcast, that people should live in such conditions, and it made me wonder that life was like this still, as if it were a hundred years ago, through an island winter. It made me wonder what a life amounted to, in the second half of the twentieth century, lived among the rocks from cradle to grave, on the eastern Atlantic coast. How might such people understand the world?*

*I set my sodden pampooties down on the large rock by my door. And as it had stopped raining now I hung the coal bags on the wall to dry as best they would and got out my broom to sweep back the estuary of dirt from my kitchen floor. Gregory came by at that moment to attend to some calves he was weaning in a little stone shed at the corner of my garden.*

*'Ah,' he said with a smile, 'you'd need to sweep your street after weather like that.'*

*Street is the yard area you have round your steading. Mine scarcely exceeds the threshold, and so is a poor excuse for a street, a joke.*

*'I've bought a pair of pampooties,' I said, by way of engaging him. He stepped across and looked sharply at them and at a glance saw that they were not a pair. They were two left feet. I had bought two left feet, he repeated.*

*'Don't you see?' and he picked them up to show me how they both laced from the same side.*

*I supposed he might think that a fool and his money are soon parted. But tonight when I called in to say hello the Feaneys were full of indignation. Gregory delayed me and Mary sat me down. It was a disgrace, they protested, to work a trick like that.*

*'A sin,' said Mary, her face flushed, 'a sin to cheat you.'*

*The thin sound of the word 'sin' seemed as much made for her lips*

*as for her character. (But she could laugh too, a mocking laugh.)*
*Wouldn't I take them back? I shrugged the matter off. It was a mistake,*
*I was sure, and said nothing of the old lady and her pipe-smoking*
*critic. She needs the money more than I do. There can't be much of a*
*trade in pampooties these days, year of our lord 1969.*


On the subject of sinners and saints, how odd it is the way they like
to haunt each other, and how the judges like to interpose themselves and point the finger. (For thou writest bitter things against
me and makest me possess the iniquities of my youth.) There were
the big holy holidays ahead, I'll allow, but otherwise I swear I
scarcely had much cause in the rest of my stay to dwell on either
saint or sinner, once St Patrick's Day was gone. Patrick's Day for
me had a treat in store, a sign taken for a wonder. I have to say I
could hardly believe it. It was a bleak, toneless kind of morning, I
remember, and cold at the fireside, with neither expectancy in the
air nor rest, except there seemed to be a disturbance, more folk in
it, to use the island expression, than usual. I hadn't been able to
make up my mind what to do. I was half in, half out, pottering,
maybe needing to escape, to run away to Galway aboard the good
ship *Naomh Eanna* for a bit of parole – 'Time off for bad behaviour' as Colm called it – at the Atlantic Hotel or the Castle if I
couldn't afford Eyre Square luxury. I was still feeling the reper-
cussions of my night of indiscretion at Dirrane's. Hard looks shot
from the garden where two brothers dug along the lane near Gort
na gCapall ready to plant their early spuds, staring up, turning
their backs, wielding their long-handled loys, as they'd like to
stove your head in, I was sure. I could even feel the edges of their

spades in the ridge of my skull. They knew I knew. I knew they knew. That one of them had called me a fool. I'd called him a fool back. All now expressed in the eyes, above a wall, across a little field, as I strode boldly by, the villain of the piece, nervous at heart, about my obscure constitutional. (Men shall clap their hands at him, and shall hiss him out of his place.) I'd have felt the same as they, which did nothing for the situation, had I been in their boots.

'Boots or no boots,' as Colm liked to say, squaring up, 'I won't put the boot in.'

She came over the wall so nimbly, I was only just aware some-one was there. I caught the movement at the corner of my eye. What was this about? Áine from the village, a young nurse on a long leave, with six eggs in a box. Synge's fare on Inishmaan, you know, was mackerel and eggs. He lived on them, his mother said. He was lucky. (He only came out in the fair months, for very short stays.) In my experience, fried eggs were the greatest culinary luxury Aran could afford, each one as rare as water in the desert. (The mackerel would have to follow for dessert, out in June. It was a lucky man who ever had the two together.)

I invited my benefactress in. She'd brought me not just six eggs but a bunch of shamrock too. She came about midday and sat till four with a great deal to say, about who was illegitimate and how, by whom, and how so-and-so had been ostracized by a stupid priest and so on. And the husband put away in the asylum at Ballinasloe. Now he was dead. How one man had dallied with another's wife, and then married her when her husband died. She questioned me about how I managed, how I survived. I said for one thing that I'd found it hard recently to order up a replacement

Calor gas cylinder from Kilronan. It was the cold snap and there being no sailings, she said. I wondered shouldn't I change to Kosan gas? Might that be a quicker service? But she said that would not do.

'That would set the cat among the pigeons, all right. What a gas!' she laughed, greatly amused at my naïveté and her pun.

One set of families had Calor gas, and another Kosan gas; grey/green cylinders versus yellow cylinders. (Big-enders, little-enders, I thought to myself, remembering my Swift, and beginning anyway to dwell on eggs.) You were on one side or the other. You could tell where each family lined up from the empty cylinders at the door awaiting collection. I said she must be joking. But no, for sure, I was wrong. Once a MacCalor, as I came to call them, always a MacCalor, never an O'Kosan. Which was she? (An O'Kosan.) It was a case of Montagues and Capulets. Did I know who the Twenties were? The who? The Twenties – that was an Aran tribe named for one of their number who went into the army. When asked to count in English he couldn't get beyond twenty. So the idea spread, with satiric venom, that this was the measure of his family, past, present and future. People called them the Twenties. They were folk to watch out for, she said, in a way that made me think she could be one of them. Was there a link between the Twenties and the O'Kosans? Which family was it boasted the celebrated abolitionist priest who campaigned through Connacht to stamp out alcohol? The O'Quixotes? I'd get to learn a lot more about it in the coming months, the hidden dynamic of that riven society, its games of vengeance and intrigue. She asked me what might have been a leading question or two. Didn't I find the Feaneys backward-looking and old-fashioned? I read danger there, perspicacious for once, and fielded it instantly, to leave her in no doubt. I did not.

And that was that, a spontaneous kindness, never anticipated, no more than it was ever repeated. I tried to think how she might have been brought to it. Had any voice been urged against it? Where had the eggs come from? How had it been decided, to give away six eggs? Or had she spirited them away from the nest-box? In which case, what had brought me to mind? Where did she get the shamrock, symbol of the trinity? After early Mass maybe, on the high road up near Oghill or away in Kilronan? In that hour or two before she made her way down the lane, what had transpired? Could it have been a sudden impulse? But what put it into her head, sudden or considered? Was this an act of spiritual diligence, some strange turn of faith and conscience, as I have seen animate people? But why? I began to wish I understood the doings of the faithful, for it seemed to me, on balance, that St Patrick had something to do with it, St Patrick patron saint of purgatory.

My pan was sizzling on the fire, as if itself salivating, the moment she'd gone. I cracked an egg on its rim, and out it swam, whitening and frittering, and making my mouth twitch and tingle as I watched it skid to a halt and film over. Never pause to ask me is there any taste in the white of an egg. Even now, I confess, when I see an egg in the pan and heading sunnily towards my plate, I thank St Patrick for the memory.

# 8

## *Crex Crex*

RIDDLE
Spring slips him in through a gap
In a stone wall, a secret agent

Bargaining with the underworld
Against sleep, a bomb

With a slow time-fuse, an old man
Winding all our clocks on, and back.

Do you know what it is? I knew what it was without ever having heard it before. Straightaway that sharp April night I knew. I was coming from the east shore – Saturday the 19th says my journal: 'Think how much of any day's not written down. Think minute by minute of the hours of solitude, in zoom-lens intensity. What solitude means. Tick, tick. Crex, crex.' And there it was, stitching its invisible way among the walls, in the growing grass. My father had described it from his Scottish boyhood often enough. The very mention of it on his lips was an elegy to the fallen world. I knew a Welshman who'd talk of hearing one beyond the hills, in Merioneth, beyond time. And who has ever seen one? Up out of the green rye, its legs dangling, wings threshing, as if it was a distant cousin of the dodo, about to forget how to fly, scraping home over the drystone wall, though it's a high flyer in reality and a speed merchant, game for a long sea-haul, from Africa or Spain. It's no land-hopper, the landrail, to give it its other name. But it's otherwise reluctant to fly and no less reluctant to be silent, day or night, but especially at night. It speaks the Latin of its species name – *Crex crex*, two-time – and goes crexing on and crexing on, ratcheting back the winding stars until you cannot see them and it's bleary-eyed dawn already. Some Celticize its note as *craik craik*. But I think the Latin onomatopoeia's more the corncrake's measure.

It seems to spend all night beneath your window, loud as a boy running a stick over and over, to and fro, along a little railing, or clacking a football rattle (now extinct), tick-tock, to and fro, across a single notch, as he sits on the bus, restless for the terraces (now no more, gone with the corncrake). It wakes you into a dream in which you hear each second tick in the mechanism of a harebrained clock. There's a breath in the curtain, the moon's a sea-green halo beyond it, and the depth-charged surf down in the bay booms and drawls accompaniment, full of the wheeling, phosphorescent notes of waders, open to infinity. Who wants to sleep anyway at a time like that? Anyone who has the dawn cow to milk, or June's spuds to spray against the blight, and the jaunting car to air and ready for the season, all in a day before night

*Crex Crex*

when *Crex crex* the crexer's about his territorial wars again, as
ineluctable and remorseless in his progress as the sands of time:

crex crex crex crex crex crex crex crex crex crex crex crex crex
crex crex crex crex crex crex crex crex crex crex crex crex
crex crex crex crex crex crex crex crex crex crex crex
crex crex crex crex crex crex crex crex crex crex
crex crex crex crex crex crex crex crex crex
crex crex crex crex crex crex crex crex
crex crex crex crex crex crex crex
crex crex crex crex crex crex
crex crex crex crex crex
crex crex crex crex
crex crex crex
crex crex
crex
crex crex
crex crex crex
crex crex crex crex
crex crex crex crex crex
crex crex crex crex crex crex
crex crex crex crex crex crex crex
crex crex crex crex crex crex crex crex
crex crex crex crex crex crex crex crex crex
crex crex crex crex crex crex crex crex crex crex
crex crex crex crex crex crex crex crex crex crex crex
crex crex crex crex crex crex crex crex crex crex crex crex
crex crex crex crex crex crex crex crex crex crex crex crex crex

'As hard to find as a four-leaf clover, the feathers very red,' Gregory will tell you.

'Kind of yellow,' Michael will decide, as you stand together down on the shore, beyond Portmurvey, and the corncrake goes at it a field away, competing with the waves, proclaiming his territory in early May.

'A queer kind of thing, short and kind of lanky-looking,' Michael will run on, in mimicry, stooping and drawing his elbows back like little wings, turning to look at me over his shoulder, with a grin, 'That kind of way … if ever you did see it,' standing up, easing his old back, 'Blink and it's gone,' dropping his jaw in feigned surprise and snapping it shut. 'Gone by the month of October too, off to Dublin … I only wish it was the same with me,' he laughs.

We peep into the field. The pocket fields are full of primroses and daisies, yellow meadow vetch and horseshoe vetch, and (dwarfed bird's foot) trefoil, violets and spring gentians, and springing grasses. The early swallows are darting through the sea-glare, zipping across the raised beach and meadow gardens. Where is the damned thing? Is it invisible? I stare and stare while Michael returns to his work, combing the strand for sea-candles, in the stiff ozone air on the tongue-sucking shingle of a hazy afternoon. I try to find a point at which to climb the wall without rattling too many rocks. But I can't, can't get into the intervening field from the shore. The corncrake falls silent, listening. But another starts up, away by the road. I'll spend a day out there, lying in the field, among the tall daisies and grasses, and still maybe never see one.

'Dr Jekyll by day, Mr Hyde by night,' I jotted. But it's not that

he's quiet by day, it's just that you notice him less. He seems row-
dier at night, a delinquent. Several delinquents, I should say, hard
at it, calling the odds, chucking their weight around. By May
they're joined by the cuckoo that's come to prey on the pipit,
gloomily boding sorrow, as the Anglo-Saxon poet said, on the
drystone skyline, magnified and amplified on a grey evening
before rain, above the Atlantic's flood-ways.

It may be that a bird we fuss about as having 'died out', like
the corncrake in Wales, is abundant elsewhere, in another country (so what's the fuss?), but its removal from our own world, its
absence, alters the place, impoverishes the hour and season. If
you belong in a place, and live in close-up, if you are local, and
have hardly ever or never been anywhere else (a rare bird yourself
in Modern Europe, in the Western World, but still such birds
existed on Inishmore in 1968 and '69), that's how it is. Everything's a familiar, a touchstone. Divinity resides in detail. You live
at the haunted heart of the mystery, of belonging, in birth and
death. Suppose the corncrake never came? Suppose the sun failed
to rise? It makes me think of a world without birds at all. Just
imagine in your own lives: no thrush on the aerial singing; no yel-
low-hammer on the droning wire, begging for a little bit of bread
and no cheese, on the empty back-roads now only of memory; no
wren's loud voice in the winter ivy; no chaffinch on the coldest
morning ever recorded for March; no wild swan whooping on the
windswept lochan; no titmice flitting on a bright spring morning,
high in the pines; no ousel deafened by the stream's spring force;
no lark ascending, nor redbreast whistling; no geese gaggling,
whiffling onto October's stubbles; no jugging nightingale to sing
in Greek; no Latin-speaking landrail, in all our little archipelago

… not a single swallow not to make a summer – just shadowy, dubious nostalgia twittering, like a dying radio signal from the redundant past, and apocalyptic ghosts soaring from the lost glades and crashing canopies of memory, rocketing on startled wings, rushing into oblivion. If ever I hear the corncrake again, one thing's for sure: if I'm not back on Inishmore, in spring or early summer, I'll be transported there at once, wherever I am, into that time-warp sound-warp of the island. But here I am only, losing my way in the wake of my notebook litter of pages, that blows eternally for me behind the *Naomh Eanna*, the ghost without the machine, stuck in 'the bank manager's' grey world. As if on waters never sailed before, as the poet Dante said.

The *Naomh Eanna* began now to bring its visitors too. As the days grew longer, tourists filled more and more of the weeks, until they seemed to throng the place, like passengers on a cruise liner that's somehow come happily to grief, run half aground on an island, now, at last, not unlike fabled Ischia, a limestone paradise, lifting a little with the tide and straining after the fleeting clouds, or then like the saint's own mysterious leviathan, eerily swathed in fogs. But first they straggled ashore, in ones or twos, wandered about for a day or two, disoriented by the wilderness wonder and stark nightmare of the place, seeming dazed and off course. Then, almost as suddenly as they'd landed, they disappeared back where they'd come from. I learnt to welcome them: they took the intensity out of our solitude, dispersed us somehow. They gave a surrealistic touch to the place, especially the plastic-mac'd folk you tended to come upon, limping about in the mist, religious types in new sweaters, pilgrims, poets, Irish, Yanks, Bretons. I learnt to resent them as intruders, as if I was a native, as we did when boys and the summer crowds of Lancastrians, Mancunians and Brummies took over the pier and the shore. Here's how I wrote to my girlfriend, after spotting my first pair, a honeymoon couple, I supposed, the way they hung about each other:

*Fishing's not been good these last few days. It's been too wild and rough. So my diet's been dull, no brainfood, as no doubt this letter will show. I've lost a lot of tackle, not enough left to set a nightline. I fish for pleasure, out of compulsion, it's my religion. I pray before the ocean. But it also helps my economies to have fish for supper or breakfast. This afternoon I had an inspiration. I'd been sweeping the kitchen floor (I lay the dust with a kettle of cold water). I do this now and then, when I'm feeling virtuous. So you know how rarely. Then I was banging some life into a cushion, the seat to my fireside chair, when I had the brainwave, the Eureka moment. The cushion's stuffed with feathers, and the quill ends of one or two hackles were sticking out through the worn embroidery. I drew one out, just idly, a long feather from low on the neck, and I knew at once what it was for. I made a little slit with my knife and picked out a few more until I had half a dozen of the right size and kind, not too curly. And there I was: I'd got the makings of some lures. I whipped three to a hook, melting some candlewax onto the whipping and rubbing it in, to grease the cotton. Then I stuck the hooks into a broken old piece of cork from a drift net, something I'd found on the shore, and put them in my pocket and off I went, with my roll of line in my other pocket. It was a sharp evening, the wind off the mainland, showing the Twelve Pins perfectly, away to the north-east, where there hung blockish, purply and orange clouds. They stood away beyond, catching the early sunset, in unreal light. Unearthly. This is an unearthly place, being so much of the ocean. So the waves chopped darkly and sprayed a little round the rocks. The island felt gloomily shadowed and somehow intensely doomy, as it can, especially on the east shore, down below Kilmurvey Bay, among the jumble of rocks there, which is where I went. (You see big rats down there sometimes, sitting on the quay at evening, taking the air when the mist's down – big as cats.) I tied and stitched a solid little rock into a bit of old net – the stuff right at the sock of a trawl – and fixed that to my line. Otherwise you have a job making a stone stay on. And with a 'dropper' of heavy nylon line – a continuation of the cord line beyond the stone – of just three feet (a little too short, but too long and it would've tangled) and one of my lures at the end of it, I began. I whirled the stone round and round my head on a couple of yards of line and then let fly, like throwing a slingshot. The line either sped out for all it was worth or snarled upon the jagged rocks and crenellations at my feet, bringing stone and lure to a dead halt in mid air. But when the stone hit the waves as intended, the current swept it along a little, delaying its descent into the depths, and gave me time to play it back at a reasonable rate, in short tugs, hand over hand, in what I judged to be a realistic enough manner, slow enough just for a fish to think the white feathers a small fish, or a sand-eel, and to snap at the hook. But what fish? I'd been doing this with periodic snarl-ups and tangles for I don't know how long – more than long enough to try most people's patience or dull their faith. The air was cold, the evening turning dark. I looked back at the bay and realized then, with a faint start, that I was being watched. How long had they been there? The young woman leant against her man to keep warm, cosily. I thought of you, the Missus ... (How can one be warm alone?) (But you won't come out here now. I hardly blame you for giving up on me, intensely lonely as sometimes I feel.) They stood there a few yards away watching. I sup-*

*pose they thought I was a native at his primitive work. But he wasn't having any luck, that native, I can tell you. And now he felt trapped by his spectators. He kept on throwing the line, untangling it from about his feet, or retrieving it from the waves, no longer believing in the enterprise but too proud to turn and go while the honeymooners (as I decided they were) stayed put. Just ten more throws, I said, and began to count down; and then ... ten more. As seems inevitable to you, but didn't seem inevitable to me, a lunge and there in the flank of a wave, the flank of a big fish, braced in the swell to resist my pull. I looked it in the eye as it held off, its blank stare. Now my problem was to get it up without it throwing the hook in some collision on the rocks. So I read the waves and kept him coming, a hand and then a hand, then a long reach and a pull to yank him ashore into a pool in a hollowed ledge just in beside me. There he was, a pollack as long as my arm, a great bar of silver and copper-gold, like nickel plate. I despatched him and assumed authority now; rolled up my line in a businesslike way, hooked my finger in at the gill of the fish, hopped across the rocks, nodded at the couple – 'Fine evening!' – and stepped out for home, fish swinging along beside me, up through the village, up by Colm's house. There he was by chance (my rival), to watch me out of sight, in the half-light, lurking round the side of his house attending to his wolfhound (a great derelict half-starved beast). I nodded at him. He acknowledged me gruffly. The big fish like a bar of silver and gold, tarnishing in the now all-but-dark, had caught his eye. I felt it was like an exchange between us, telling him something about me he didn't know. Then as I came away I heard the corncrake. The corncrake supplanted even my fish, in that moment, throwing the night into another gear, catching my heart, sweeping me starward. I stood until the stars came out, as if the noise would stop and I'd never hear*

*it again, caught in the long roar of the sea and the cold air. Crex crex*
*crex crex crex ...*


It was that night, as I say, that I became aware of the corncrake. It was that night, too, word was sown that I was a fair kind
of fisherman, and the night, for me, that really heralded the onset
of serious fishing. They were still early days, but it was spring
now, at last. This is where a wiser man would have chosen to
begin his story. But who knows whether he'll be a wise man or a
fool? Things were changing. The crexer was on the march, the
long march to daybreak. And I was on a new march of my own,
with fish to fry shoaling in my mind's eye, a new diet, and a great
stay against the bank. There was more on that fish than I could
eat in two meals; and more, to be plain, than I wanted to eat,
because the pollack's one of the least toothsome fish I know
(though it's caviar to the general run of wrasse, that other
standby, let me say at once). The islanders seem to like pollack,
though. (Sometimes I caught so many I could hardly carry them
all home to give away.) In Wales they used to call them 'coalies'
(coalfish). Old ladies in the village bought them for their cats and
stank the house out, stewing them of flavour. But at last,
inevitably, I had to re-equip myself. I had been rash in setting
lines when the sea was still too wild to tolerate them, or when the
ripped-up weed would so entangle them they became worthless,
and though I continued to fish with my line and feather lures for
a few more days (with a little hard-won success), I began to look
ahead and made a shopping list, thinking to the summer proper
when there'd be more fish to catch than I could cope with, when
there'd be mackerel (and the rare egg, maybe). I reckoned it was

worth the money to make another trip to Galway to buy some more and better tackle.

A decisive trip it proved, in quite unguessable ways. How many times have you been with me to Galway now? In dire straits and other? Didn't I tell you, the *Naomh Eanna*'s part of island life, and Galway part and parcel? So it was this time, for when I jumped aboard – Wednesday, 23 April – I found myself not down among the pigs but in the midst of a wedding party. An islander from one of the big families was to marry a mainland girl. I didn't record, or didn't know, what day the marriage was solemnized, as they say. Solemnity seemed to pass me by. But I suppose it must have been one of the weekdays, rather than the coming Saturday, for we all seemed to sail back again on Saturday morning. I say it was the Saturday; it might have been Monday. Last Monday of the month enjoyed a sailing, for Tuesday's market. Saturday was what I put down. I believe there was Mass next day. I was in no fit state, let me advise you, when I got to bed the night of my return to know or to remember, or to care, what day, month, or year it was we sailed and the happy couple tied the knot. I was on a rare old voyage of my own, climbing the cruel high seas of a hangover from hell, every crest a creamy reminder of too many pints. Nor was I any use the next day, or the day after that. When I booked in that outward night at the Castle Hotel, I was lucky to find a bed because of the wedding crowd. In the end I had it only on the understanding that I'd have to share ... with whomever it was. I felt, as I lay there, as if I'd stepped into the opening pages of *Moby-Dick*, and was as exercised as Ishmael at the prospect, thinking I must pass my nights sharing my room, if not my bed, with ... With whom? Some savage Aran MacQueequeg harpooner? But no one materialized on the first night or the second night. They were too busy celebrating, I supposed.

On Friday, or, by now, Saturday morning, things briefly boded not too well. Someone stumbled in and lurched around the room a while, banging against my bed, feeling the air with a hand. I lay still. They were fighting in the bar below. I could hear the furniture breaking and the cries and shouts beneath my room. (Colm's meaning of parole, but he'd stayed home; the Galway landlady's meaning of savagery.) Then the intruder stumbled out. And so my last night went and no one disturbed me more than that, and no one mistook my bed for his, or for a urinal. And no one settled any score. For which I had always to be on the lookout since Dirrane's.

Next day was like the first day of summer, in the first summer of your innocence, brisk and bright, fast with seabirds and chopping waves. We ran home, at a pelt, straight to Kilronan, the bar full, showband music blaring, trailing gaily behind us with the gulls. Because there's nothing new under the sun, I thought this time I'd stay in the saloon and join the throng in drinking away the journey. So from shortly after half-past-eight to one-thirty when we landed, I downed a fair few bottles of Guinness. (I've never had an epic capacity but I soon lost count of how many that day.) Then one thing ashore led to another. It was such a beautiful day, it needed no enhancement, but nonetheless called contagiously for celebration. We disembarked and dispersed to McDonough's, Conneely's American, or Kenny's, according to our tribal affiliations. There was much I did and do remember of that day, in detail, as seems to be my way. Hard to forget, for it attracted a lot of attention on the quay, was a Norwegian shark-fishing boat, barbed fore and aft with harpoon guns, and the wild-looking but silent Norwegian crew themselves, found in the corner at Conneely's, drinking Phoenix lager, in sure and certain hope of resurrection.

'Piss,' as Colm said, sidelong, 'horsepiss', burying his head in the next black pint.

There was quite a business going on at that time, harpooning basking sharks, for the oil in their livers, I believe. The liver of a thirty footer can weigh 2,000 lbs, someone said. (It was one of the several wholly unrealistic things Robert Flaherty had his men of Aran do, killing sharks from an open boat, putting their lives at risk to make his movie *Man of Aran*. You only have to have set eyes on a full-grown, hulking basking shark – a big one can be between forty and fifty feet long and contain a ton of plankton in its belly – to understand the hazard they were set, high sea or not.) Aran fishermen, they said, were to supply basking sharks that summer to scientists in Dublin, for research into heart disease. Too little exercise, too much basking? But generally the talk wasn't so knowledgeable or informative. I'd fallen in to drinking with Colm and a near neighbour of mine, the old crone Maggie's brother Tam Faherty. He was retired from a life on the trawlers, a gangling old man of scarce a word but with a wide gleaming eye, a smile and laughter, ever at the ready, to lubricate his oath of *omertà*. There was one of the O'Kosans with us too, a lobsterman who fished from Kilmurvey. He told Colm, and some other fellow leaning at the bar, to leave me alone, when Colm began to get edgy with me, as he liked to do. (Though I was a MacCalor by tenanthood, the O'Kosans were good to me. They'd brought me shamrock and eggs, and now protection.)

We drank on into the afternoon, the talk mostly in Irish,

occasionally switched for my benefit into English, about wedding capers, gossip, who'd done what at the Castle (and to whom), what the winter's fishing had been like, and the prospect of the coming lobster season. We emerged at about four-thirty, shadows now falling on Kilronan hill. We stood about, drunkenly deciding what to do next, and in the meantime, Colm squared up in front of me and demanded a fight. (A few months later I met an island man who *begged* me for a fight, pleaded for it on his mother's grave. That was when I realized, too late to oblige with Colm, that this fighting business wasn't so much about fighting as about friendship. You get your head kicked in and I'll be your brother. Who'd have guessed?) We ran through his usual pre-fight talk, Marquis of Queensberry rules, no use of the head, no use of the boot … And so I thought, well, let him throw the first punch, if he must, and stood before him, watching (swaying probably too, with the quantity of drink I'd downed). But he wouldn't – pride wouldn't let him begin – and if he wouldn't start I wasn't going to, which wound him up till he could hardly bear it. He swore and bristled and burned with anger, wanting to fight so much. Then we all set off for home in Colm's five-hundred-weight van.

We got no farther than his house, where his mother and his sister invited me to share their dinner of potato stew. They were the poorest people I knew, poorer than any in the village, as poor as any even in landless Killeany, their house bare of any comfort, bare of carpet, threadless, drafty, empty, rattling. Yet Colm had his van, it was true, and money for drink (as any moralizing holy Willy might observe), and kept a half-starved wolfhound that could eat as much as a man. I can't tell you how much I enjoyed

my supper and accompanying hospitality, no matter that my head
was dazed and stomach raw for food. I saw that at last I was closing somehow with Colm, hothead that he was, or so it felt, and
the tragedy of his family, the harsh lot fate and the priesthood
had dealt him, and the provocation I must be, idling around.

Colm explained it to me how once the houses, white cabins,
had stood together along the sloping lane, and the world was different, and his family had prospered. It was a shaming reminder
to him to talk about it and, as who would not be, he was bitter.

'We live like tenants in a slum now, like tinkers off the road.
Holes in our boots, or no boots.'

But now Tam passed the window and was waiting for us at
the door. We left soon enough, swerving all three of us back again
to Kilronan, and a few pints more, at Kenny's this time. We
drank them out of doors, standing on the street, backs against the
wall (to stop us falling down). Then Colm and Tam decided we'd
go out west. They'd got a curragh there and we'd take it across to
the Callagh, out beyond Bungowla, to the Brannogues, to check
some lobster pots, the first of the season. They judged it safe to
go, there being no break in the weather as night fell. There are
roads you take, once taken, from which you can't retreat, drunken
roads that spring like genies from a bottle to spirit you away.
They're upon you as much as you're upon them. They're marked
with headstones for milestones, the tragic graves of fallen youth,
rural victims of Saturday night who ran the gauntlet of the gods
and died, as though their souls were weary of their lives.

We rattled along as the sun set and sank itself beneath the
cliffs and under the sea, sinking us in shadow, a world suddenly
gloomy as Guinness dregs, on the landward shore, the land of

darkness and the shadow of death. Up and down the wild road we ran, drunk, among the walls and terraces, back to Bungowla.* There I'd last been blasted through to the skin by rain. This time I was blasted inside out by a skinful of the dark backward and abysm of time gentlemen please, in a land where time was never called. But your number might be up, on such a night, in the turbulent strait across to the Callagh. We rattled down as near to the Sound as we could and parked up. A dogend of sun still smouldered faintly in the waves, away across the ocean. A couple of curraghs lay just off the track, sleek bellies up, beetle-black. Beside them, among the boulders, some old-style islander had claimed a pile of driftwood by crowning it with a rock. Colm was in a hot mood. After scarce a quick look round, he toppled the pile with his boot and violently slung the timber into the back of his van.

The three of us now raised one of the curraghs up and got under it, Tam under the stern, Colm amidships and me beneath the bow. And then we headed off. The prow of a curragh rises proud and high from the sea. Consequently, when it's overturned and you're under it, as part of a pantomime beetle, it closes down your view ahead far more than it might otherwise. You can scarcely see even the rocks beneath your feet, let alone the ground ahead, especially when the man at the stern is as tall as Tam Feaney. The rocks may be dry at first, but as you cross the tidemark they get wetter, and they get weedier, and slipperier. We began smartly in full strides down the strand, arms up, heads

---

*It wasn't so long before that Gregory had warned me not to go out there 'on account of the lunatic Pádraig O'Toole' – Father O'Toole – back from Nigeria with a rifle and shooting it in all directions.

down, seats banging on our necks, hands gripping, rocks rattling underfoot. Colm urged us on, until we were at a run, rock-hopping perilously down the steep shore. He lunged, upping the pace, as we hit the last and worst rocks. If he couldn't punch my lights out he might run them out and crack a shin or a break an ankle, I thought, but I hopped and sprang along as best I could and kept my end up, just, until we could only stop, or drown, beside the sharp current, sliding to a halt on the black weed, tilting her over onto her keel, and taking stock while Tam went off to bring down the 'sticks'.*

Colm pointed out where we were going, but apart from showing the general direction of our course it wasn't clear, because the Brannogues lay in inky shadow, how far we'd have to row, or on what seas. The moon in a gauze of cloud was coming like a bleary bride round Crahalaun. Now we pushed off like the last men embarked to find America, even later than Columbus, who, as we all know now, was the last one to make it, but yet won fame's silver teapot. Might we be rewarded with the runner-up's lobster? The air was full of the Atlantic's wide and restless roar. The current in the strait ran deep and black, eddying here and swirling as we cut across, deeper than hell. Gulls ghosted by, eerie in the darkness. We scarcely rose and scarcely fell, but now and then felt the current on us broadside, like a warning from the Styx, that we passed by under sufferance, by a rescindable dispensation. I was surprised how much the bladeless sticks could catch and how we sped or turned and how the laths of the curragh pulsed and quivered. I was amidships and measured my pull and pace with Tam's.

*There's a slipway now at Bungowla but there were only rocks there in my day.

I had rowed on the sea before and in my youth played ghillie to my father all the livelong day, as he fly-fished for trout on Llyn Cefni out on Môna's isle. It was nothing to me to row, except to row with others in such a barque, in a whirlpool of Guinness, in a narrow strait, with the moon rising and the surging Atlantic Ocean stacked like a staircase away to America.

As we came closer to the Callagh – an inlet in the main Brannogue island – my sense of peril grew. The ocean, now to port, towered and collapsed, surging back on itself, waltzing like a drunk, taking a deep step back and sideways for every step forward. It should have ripped straight at us through the channel and swept us down, scattering our sticks in the air. But at low tide like this it tripped itself up invisibly on rocks below. Otherwise we'd have been blown away to Connemara or more likely run over and drowned, sent flying to a watery grave, lost with all hands, three souls overboard, not a stick washed ashore, our bones hurled beyond stormy Donegal. We would have been as though we had not been. Who'd know we were gone or how? Until the morning, when they'd guess – the van on the road, the curragh missing and us not home? It was the old old story, the traditional fate of riders to the sea. The skyscraper American waves couldn't reach us but it was sobering to see them and hard just to trust they'd continue to sink back down and not follow through. So I pulled my sticks and prayed, sober enough to pray, in the name of anyone or anything, until we found the stillness of the Callagh and hunted for the marker buoy upon the moonlit water.

The pots were empty but for a few crabs. It seemed like Colm's luck. He cracked the crabs on the gunwale, tossed them broken, overboard, back to the sea floor, the bottom of the monstrous world, and baited up again. Then we rowed back into the night, the moon now merely marbled and drifting smokily, like the ghost of the flame on the Statue of Liberty's torch. With each stroke, the drink weighed increasingly upon us, a spring tide pulled by the moon, as the adrenalin of our setting out subsided. They left me to bring the sticks and marched the curragh up together. Six sticks, with their wooden flange-thole-pin holes, make awkward luggage and I slipped and fell with them clattering about my head, once, and then again until, face down in the seaweed, bruised and battered, I couldn't even raise myself to my knees. I licked the dust. I lay there in the darkness. I could hear Colm and Tam talking up on the road and then after a while Colm calling me to hurry up. I heard him as the boxer on the canvas hears the count pass nine. Colm had had his day. Then somehow I got up and he and Tam at last came staggering to the rescue, and took the sticks, or so I seem to remember. And home we must have gone, for there I found myself shipwrecked on my bed: my head full of monster corncrakes, grating round and round, next day, and the day after. More corncrakes in my head than there are stars in the sky or stones on Aran.

# 9

## In Memory of Christy Mahon

As it turned out, I could not have plotted things better, if I had wanted to enrich my tale, by composing the letter myself, with its foregone conclusion, and passing it off for real. Not that I am claiming to be sufficiently inventive to pass things off for real. I am just a word-bitten plodder as you know, on the low sea-road of a poor man's genre, scarce Christy Mahon's shadow cast at noon. I touch my cap to you folk above, on the high road, poets and scholars. (Fine evening …) But there it was. My father had decided to pursue me. Was he still reeling from the wound in the head I'd given him, chucking up my career as I had? He wrote and I had no option to turn him back. He was already on his way, thanks to a storm and a delay in the mails. He'd be coming with his bosom crony, his trusty fishing partner, Meirion. Meirion was hearer and heartener, key mentor of my youthful reading in the poets (who have so much to answer for: Hopkins, Owen, Kavanagh, MacDiarmid, Thomas, Thomas, and Thomas). And then there was, to

understand, his teasing scorn for that villain of cultural imperial-
ism, Matthew Arnold (who has, to a Cymro, so much to answer
for). Meirion worked as an artist for a branch in North Wales of a
Dublin advertising company called McConnell's. He was very
poorly paid. He was a true unheroic hero, a bard and autodidact,
a private far-from-royal Welsh fusilier, a post-colonialist *avant la
lettre*. He and my father had collaborated on books. Scotch whisky
tempered by lyrical Welsh water, they were a great complement in
company. Who could have anticipated better companions?

I, for one. I couldn't believe my eyes. Nor could I believe, as
the scales fell from them, that here I was caught in a comic parody. Here I was at the crucifying crux that had come to test poor
Christy Mahon. His heroic boast had been that he'd killed his
father with a loy – let fall the edge of it on the ridge of his skull,
so he fell down like an empty sack. Is it me? What did I have to
do to be myself in the world, to rid myself of the past? Not step
back? Close with it? We'd been so close, my father and I. I'd
walked behind him from the age of ten, right through my adolescence and beyond, high into the wilderness of the eastern
Carneddau to fish the remotest lakes he could find. He was a
magnetic wonder to a boy and youth (and is a wonder to me now,
on the low road of octogenarian being as he is, in and out of the
ditch), a compelling storyteller, with a poet's ear and a poet's eye,
no time for claptrap, or lip-service, a man of and for the people,
an inveterate republican, but never a party-man, keenest of all to
fish the wilds or talk or dream about it (an Honorary Doctor now,
of Glasgow University). I'd be his retriever when he shot Lord
Mostyn's pheasants or a freakish hare. I'd be his runner,
despatched with the gun, to hunt out any edible flesh or fowl that

crossed our rocky, wooded little bit of land, our bryn at the town's
border, and seldom failed him. I'd climb the limestone crags to
bring us gulls' eggs for breakfast, to service his nostalgia and
found my own. He showed me just once when I was a small boy
how to set a snare, at what height, in what places, and off I went
and caught a rabbit first time. He had an extra sense for such
things, and he saw I had it too. My weekends and holidays I
spent toiling, moiling, digging at his bidding, or skulking with a
gun in crepuscular woods … and, as you know, fishing, in an
Eden, but an Eden that fell as rapidly as my sap rose, an Eden I
knew somehow I had to escape, a double-edged Eden. Yet
though I could leave it, I didn't seem capable of escaping it or
keeping it from haunting me. I could take myself out of the
dream but not the dream out of myself. There was always the
spectre of it to pursue me in books. I found it everywhere, in any
number of pages, more than a spectre, a rooted thing. I didn't
know how to sever and discard it, to enter the metropolis where
modern life goes on maturely, any more than I knew how to go
about the world without a head. All this you know but the
prospect of a paternal visit pressed it home again upon me. In my
generation, at least, you need to be old, and lucky, before you can
revisit the father-son relation comfortably.

I had even begun my career just as the old man had done,
writing news. Now I wanted that impossibility: to become my
own man. I might have thought I was seeking community among
the wilderness's poor and to write about their world as best I
could. I believed it true, as George Crabbe said, and believe it
now, that what forms the real picture of the poor demands a song,
however finely self-promotional the witness, better the song than

silence, if better still sixpence in a poor bugger's pocket. But really wasn't I just postponing the hour, the reckoning (the reckoning at the bank, if in no higher court)? Not singing, but sinking?

So the old man's kindly, uncritical, merely functional letter yet seemed to prompt me to question and suspect. It was so unanticipated it came with a shock, a punch in my lights. I seemed to see, as I set the letter down on the kitchen table, hand quivering a little, and looked out at the Atlantic sky, that I was doing nothing but regressing, holding out against responsibility. Was I (am I not still?) a victim of words and books merely, and are books just an excuse for living, living things out in parenthesis, even in that most desolate stony place as I was, quotations and misquotations raining down on me thick and fast – words, words, words – the multitude of words, a parody of rain? For after all, as old Mrs Feaney said, the rain is healthy. And the rain it raineth everyday. But the stuff of books and solitude and spying on the poor, could they be healthy? Or were my doubts the real heresy and treason? What book ever changed the world? It seems a solipsism to say that what changes the way we see the world, changes the world, but it is not. Where do you want me to begin? The Bible, *Das Kapital? The Divine Comedy, The Satanic Verses*? But to get back onto the low road, after pausing to look at the navigational stars: like Christy Mahon, to keep within the bounds of a book, I had my own little lie to live with, my even more farcical boast to live down. He'd as much killed his father, as it turned out, as I had got a wife. What sweet poetic justice had befallen me, what an O'Freudian petit master-script in the art of exposing MacOedipus: the return of the father, books or no books, boots or no boots, trouble afoot.

Is it me? They clearly didn't think so. I stood there, bold as you like, not hanging back, on the quayside, in battered old trousers and boots, Aran sweater next my skin, raw and warm in the cold, with a rusty beard (which is what threw them, I suppose). But they couldn't recognize me, even when they were off the gangway. I had to step towards them and all but tug the old man by the sleeve and say it was me, the prodigal. (You?) Who'd have expected that? In all the time it took the *Naomh Eanna* to sidle up and open the rail, they'd searched the faces ashore on the gusting jetty and failed to know me. I could have been anyone. What had become of me? I felt refreshed by my performance, my little liberty.

There were in fact three of them. A great tall gentleman was with them – gentleman was the name for him – a man with a face like a shovel, in a trenchcoat mac and a racegoer's trilby hat of brown felt, a man of large gesture and big brown brogues: Charles E. McConnell, the man whose business kept our Meirion poor. He was to stay at a guesthouse. The other two were to stay with me. It was late May now, Saturday the 24th. The weather had broken and it had rained all day the day before, soaking and blackening the land. An easterly wind now blew strong and cold. My visitors met Aran in grey-black bleak mode. It was the third degree of grey, the interrogating grey, softened only by light-catching puddles and rain-glinting stone, and they seemed pensive. Perhaps they'd been subdued by a brisk crossing and were out of focus. I had to take care as we came down the harbour road to warn them about the 'Missus', just in case anything emerged to take them by surprise. Gregory being busy on the land, I'd recruited Michael and his mare Molly to drive us back, to a lunch of mutton stew, spuds, turnips, and tinned peas, and booked them again for a run that evening, out to Bungowla, to give my guests a chance to see the length of the place in all its extremity and splendour. The breadth we explored on foot by ourselves next day, just the three of us (Charlie McConnell being racked by sciatica and at death's door from the jolts and joys of jaunting in a cold east wind). The old man looked at me and laughed, and seemed to take the Missus in his stride, as if he understood it didn't matter. He seemed more concerned that I neither looked nor sounded like myself. (Do you realize, he'd ask me later, that you sound just like these people? When in Rome, I said, ever the chameleon, ever the lyrebird, ever the Gulliver.) But for now the greater part of my visitors' attention was distracted by the strange sights and sounds about them, as the islanders bustled to take ashore the usual fare from the steamer. (The sea-chastened beauty of the *Naomh Eanna*, as I saw her again, blowing and shipshape, tugging to be free and footloose, off down the islands next, made me wish I could stow away and write the story of her life.) And they had more than enough to turn their heads as we travelled the road home, all clipped with cold on the high car, over the back of Aran.

In that mood on Inishmore, in a grey study, desolation and melancholy seem irresistibly to close upon each other, to blow your mind. That night I braved Dirrane's (like entering a hostile saloon in a western) to bring a dozen-and-a-half pint bottles home in a sack and the three of us sat in candlelight before the hearth, drinking and talking. There was the perennial nationalism v. internationalism argument, Meirion being for one, my father being for the other; and I? I was neither for nor against either. My line was to pray for the universal withering away of institutionalized religion.

'Who has it harder, would you say, father or son? You've both been both, so maybe you know?' I slurred my absurd question, apropos of what I failed to scribble down.

'The son,' said my father, with feeling.

'The son?' quizzed Meirion.

'The son, because the father should know better, having himself been a son. Because the father has the upper hand ... And God damn him to hell if, like mine, he uses it to beat a child ... I'd piss on his grave. And after that,' the old man, no Christian, paused, with a chuckle, 'the Holy Ghost. The Holy Ghost has it hardest of all.'

'The sin against the Holy Ghost, what is it?' said Meirion, 'Louis MacNeice, you know ... In the Bible, Abraham ...' he re-embarked.

'Abraham!' I mocked, 'Abraham and Isaac. God Almighty and Jesus Christ! That's such a terrible story, isn't it, an outrageous story? What sane lesson could there be in it? ... But I don't mean just nasty like that, primitive and savage, I mean hard and hardest in every decent sense to bear?'

'In the name of the Father,' said my father, half to himself, as if in no certain connection, but maybe in sorry reflection at what had become of me, 'who's to say? Old men become very crude in their cunning, or perhaps they fancy that younger men are necessarily simple?'

My guests were weary from their travels and the bottles died fast, sinking with the candles and driftwood flames, only six pints each, and nothing in the house for the road but some sweet medicinal rum. Before retreating to bed, we paused at the door and stood in the foggy damp, to hear the muffled corncrake, starless, without compass point, or map reference, beating his bounds, staking new claims. If it brought a tear to my father's eye to hear it, I cannot say I saw it, for the dark. Meirion began quietly to hum 'Ar lan y môr …' and then, as if for effect, 'Hen wlad fy nhadau.'

'Land of my fathers,' muttered my father.

'What I need is a woman,' I said, startling myself with my own words, as if among my benighted peers, as we peed into the pitch black together.

'That's what you think you need,' said the old man.

'A woman?' asked Meirion, quizzically, 'Do you know, I don't think, since I was a young man in Bala …'

And he was off on one of his typical excursions, leading us round in laughter, by inconsequence after inconsequence (which brother's sister had an artificial leg, of so light an alloy it used to blow from under her in a high wind and bring her crashing down upon her arse – most unfortunate; who fell in the lake on Christmas eve and what she wasn't wearing; whose widowed third cousin twice removed gave birth to twins and would never name the father), to the iniquities of the English Empire (home and abroad), the Monarchy and other attendant parasites, the Prince of Wales (that year invested), the English Public School system, Oxbridge, the Civil Service, Whitehall, the Judiciary, and the House of Lords … and still no sight of a woman emerging naked from Llyn Tegid. Meirion died over eighty, and enjoyed a public funeral, with crowds of Welsh folk in the street, descended from near and far, to hear his pre-recorded oration, *ave atque vale* at his own tomb, on a PA system, a man of steady cool in the face of death. But he died too soon to see the old establishment he loathed begin, at last, to teeter at the brink of oblivion.

The cymbal rang at my door. I made the porridge for the morning. The candles guttered, gasping to be snuffed, and snuffed they were, and off at last we went to bed. My guests seemed to understand my madness. I lay there listening to them clattering about, to the unfamiliar creak of old bedsteads, of company of any kind bigger than a mouse overhead or guttersnipe starling in the eves, day or night. I lay there wondering when shall I rise and the night be gone? So I might scribble them up in my journal, in quick sketchy notes, pinning down particulars. I learnt much later how my visitors had been shocked by what they had found, by the spartan and frugal way I lived (on wateriest of watery mutton stews while they were there) and the intensity of the island's desolation. The sun broke through next day and brightened up the evening but they hardly saw the island at its most idyllic. On their departure (Monday, 26 May, B-sailing for Tuesday's Galway Fair, depart 1 p.m.), on a day of limpid leaden beauty, my father won the Feaneys' highest praise. He was, Mrs Feaney said, 'a plain man' (indeed he'd started life a peasant as much as they, on a remote Scottish steading). I knew as she said it what she meant without saying. A man may become respectable, as we know, by having a father and telling a decent lie.

Respectable or not, I watched out as ever, as best I could, against being set upon on the road at night. But I still became nocturnal, as need was, as the days grew long (light at eleven) and the tides swung round, and I fished with various methods and techniques, nightline and handline, supplying myself, and often the Feaneys, with plenty of pollack and one or two small mackerel. We had some terrible unfishable weather just after the old man's visit, rain day after day, blackening everything, and wind, and gloom, as if we were back in January, just when I needed to be busy, to shrug off the after-shocks and disturbances caused by the embassy from Wales. They'd made me think how time had flown, how time was running out, and what to do when it stopped?

Then the weather brightened and settled and, as if reading both the skies and my mind, the old man sent me out an old fibreglass five-foot spinning rod and reel, together with a box of lures, tackle I'd used in my youth to kill mackerel on the western rocks beyond Gogarth. That made things look up. The best spot for mackerel nearby was down below the Atlantic cliffs at the edge of Blind Sound, at low and rising tide. You could get there with time-consuming effort, ten-league rock-hopping almost to Gort na gCapall, and tracking back on the surf-pounded ledge, rock all pocked with pools, and hard to cross, beyond Poll na bPeist, way down below, to the Sound. But if you had just a little courage you could climb down the cliff at a particular point where it wasn't at its highest and there were accessible ledges to traverse in relatively easy steps below. It took me a while to face it and step back off the edge, and make the one telling move, to round a little buttress, that left you exposed to the swirling sea and the rocks below, at no tremendous height (fifty or sixty feet?), but more than enough to put paid to you, were you to slip, one little slip of fingertips or toes, after rain when the rock was wet. (You needed a pair of pampooties maybe, left-foot and right-foot?) You would not survive, even if you plunged straight into the sea, without clouting a rock, because there you'd drown, drawn by the currents, numbed and battered by the waves.

After a few tense and frozen refusals, I soon became adept at this route, carrying my rod along as well, and sometimes on the way up my catches too, but they were slipperier and usually it seemed wiser to go the long way home, or I might lose them, or fall snatching after them. I spent many trance-like hours down there, dreaming the world into being, in the full sea glare. The ancient fort of Dún Aengus loomed away above, and the cliff-haunting seabirds, whirring razorbills and whizzing guillemots, zipped in and out, gulls wheeled and made their arcs or fluttered into waves to snatch pollack, gulping them whole as they rose again; terns skimmed and beating hung, to plummet after white-bait, and gannets, when they came, nose-dived like kamikaze fighter planes. And there I stood, in all their combined cacophony, at the edge of the rushing, dazzling sea, tide after tide, at the edge of the western world.

Once a demon seventh wave nearly snatched me to my grave. But I threw myself down, in an adrenalin instant, onto hands and knees, as it sprang and crashed. Aerated like giant champagne, it surged high over me. I clutched my rod as if for dear life. But, for dear life literally, I gripped the barnacled pinnacles and cutting crenellations of rock. There was time to think, as always in life-threatening crises of the kind. I felt like a bizarre crustacean, bracing not to succumb to the huge sucking backwash that when at last it came would have swept me away and written my obituary in the waves. My palms and forearms were cut, when I surfaced, and ankles, knees and shins all grazed. I had inherited a cocker spaniel by then, bequeathed, unwanted, to the Feaneys by some relations in Galway who'd spoiled it, and the dog liked to follow me everywhere. The sea took him that sunny afternoon, tumbled him and terrified him, drove him rolling right back, battered and cut about the nose, to the base of the cliff. I thought I'd never see him again. After the experience, he refused to come down with me, but sat and looked down from the top of the cliff, hour after hour, as long as I took retreating from the tide, head cocked at my every move, waiting for me, watching for me, like a land-bound seal, head above the waves. Rover he was called, but the sea tamed his roving, a wild rover no more, poor beast.

The mackerel came there, off the southern point of the horseshoe, in enormous shoals, big enough to make the hair stand on your neck. I remember the night I first saw them. The day was failing fast and the slack tide calm as a millpond, slurping, sucking, but never breaking. It was dank and gloomy down there on the rocks, a little eerie, a little unsettling, a little cold, once the day rounded the high fort. If you paused to think of conger eels, you could hear them bark, and come lunging at you from under some weed-glugging overhang, with the ferocity of crocodiles, to bite off your face (as my father told me had happened once to a man probing under rocks for lobsters, below Penmaen). I was still using my handline then and catching only pollack, when the mackerel came in a shoal a hundred yards wide and as deep as a three-storey house, deeper than the eye can see in even such clear water, a squad of helmeted militia, inch-perfect in their drill, like Red Square on May Day, or a Nuremberg rally, or riot police on high alert in the Paris streets of '68. Naïvely I raised my arm to throw my line – like a revolutionary with a Molotov cocktail on its sling – thinking I couldn't miss. But in the instant my arm went up, the thoroughbred shysters turned themselves inside out, turned on their tails and sped, like a startled flock of birds, thousands of them, in their phoney tiger stripes and metallic blue-green armour. Bully-boys in number, brave in the face of whitebait. The sea rioted with them, boiled in an instant, resounding as if hit by the briefest imaginable ambush of automatic fire, a hundred thousand shots in a nanosecond, and then was calm again. Dara from Gort na gCapall, with whom I fished down there on many evenings (who gave me the Irish priest's elegy to the drowned young men of Killeany), told me how it was: when the mackerel first came, their eyes were sharp as fishhooks, needle sharp, but as the days wore by the sunlight made them blind.

'So, don't you see, you can catch the buggers on nothing, by the month of August, on a white shirtbutton and a knot of line.'

It was Dara who taught me my mackerel times-table:

3 mackerel = one hand

40 hands = one hundred (120)

to each 'hundred' add a 'tilly hand' = one for good luck or measure

£3.00 a hundred was a good price at that time.

Dara caught his mackerel and cured them in a barrel for the winter, a layer of mackerel, a layer of salt, a layer of mackerel, etc., etc.

For myself, I had no need for many fish, just fish day by day, because I had no means to keep them cool and fresh, and in the muggy summer climate milk went off, fish went off, meat went off, in an instant. So I did fish almost every day or night, if the weather permitted, and as the tides dictated, just for the day in hand, though often it was hard to stop, and several times I saw the dawn awaken at my back and silver the sea with light. Away ahead of me in America the world would be asleep or just going to bed, exiles from Aran among them, dreaming of what?

At this time, inspired by the trip to the Callagh with Colm and Tam, I spent some hours repairing the frame of the stoved-in lobster pot I'd had since winter, jetsam you'll recall I stashed away, hoping to add a little luxury to my diet. With hazel wands and withies and wire and old net from the shore, I restored it, until it looked as if it might work and be robust enough to survive a tide or two. Then I waited for the first tide that would be slack out at one in the morning or so, when no one would see me, trudging to the shore with the barrel pot on my back, ready baited with two halves of a wrasse tied fast with wire. The pot was awkward and quite unevenly heavy, weighted as it was by three clumps of cement set in along its base. I had to struggle to manage my lamp as well, on a circuit from our village least likely to bring me to anyone's attention, should anyone be about, after a late night's drinking.

I took the back lane from Kilmurvey, crossed the road and backtracked to the lane that led to the raised strand beyond Portmurvey. Would it be worth the effort? I always seemed to believe doggedly on such crackpot ventures that if I could imagine the end result I could obtain it. I lit the lamp. At first, as you know, a lamp in the open, under only a tattered net of stars, blinds you and seems more a hindrance than a help. But once my sight settled, closed inside the centre of its penumbra, I edged out towards Craghalmon, stepping with care into the drunken arc of light ahead of me, dragging the pot over the slippery weedy patches, then to-ing and fro-ing between lamp and pot, advancing in stages over the outcrop rocks, until I reached the sucking and slopping, sombre limits of the tide, all in the cool night air and small, seething night-sounds of the open shore. Then I had to go back up to the strand to find a rock of a good shape for an anchor. So I slipped and slid back and forth until ready to look for the ideal trough, a deep narrow, into which I could sink the pot with hope of retrieving it after the tide had done its work, or somewhere to wedge it, that I might return to, and I could not find one. Of course I also wanted a promising spot, where there might be a lobster. I mustn't lose sight of the object of the exercise. But that was something I could only guess at.

What did I know about lobsters? Little more than how good they are to eat. I went slithering around, wary of the glugholes, probing as best I could the great locks of weed that draped the rocks and swirled around as the sea sucked. It would be easy enough to release the pot, to let it slide down until it stopped, but was it going to do any good there? And would I ever be able to drag it out? It began to seem a harebrained idea, a wild-lobster chase. I'd thought I knew where to set it but now I couldn't make up my mind. I moved on along the shore. I moved back. The tide began to slurp more actively. In the end, because the sea was turning now, brimming at its outer limits, and I was anyway beginning to lose faith, I settled on a little cleft and wedged the pot into it, anchoring its tether by jamming the rock under the lip of a heavy boulder nearby. Then off to bed to sleep away the tide, dreaming of ragged claws scuttling across the silent seabed, excitedly parting the weed, in search of breakfast. On several days I slept till noon or four or six to wake up with the tide (only once to an all but shell-less purple lobster, the choicest delicacy; several times to crab), or to catch up with the clock, when coming back into orbit, as out in July the astronauts returned from walking about on the Aran-scape of the moon.

For it wasn't all fishing and sleeping in and holidays now for me. I whitewashed my cabin. I began to go about more with Gregory, at first in tandem with his brother Bartley, then just the pair of us. They hired me in for my daily fare to help them haul the hay and rye. I'd waited a long time to come to know Gregory better. I was shy and awkward and he was awkward and impatient. Besides, he was such a daybreak-to-nightfall workaholic, always haring off, here, there and everywhere, to attend sheep or cattle, and his crops of hay and rye and spuds. He owned, it seemed, a hundred and one pocket fields up and down the island, as many, I used to think, as there are stars in the sky. When he wasn't in one he was in another, or on the road at dawn, bareback on the Big Fella, the morning fresh with the scent of the sea and rattling with hooves as he passed. For the most part, he and his brother held land round our village. Neither had much time for talk or idling. Bartley was the more relaxed, the sunnier character, a married man. He'd take time out to go to the centenary meeting of the Galway Races, coughing epidemic or no coughing epidemic, and he'd greet you with laughter. Did you win? 'I did!' Did you get good odds? 'Great odds,' he'd say, 'great odds, entirely.' But Gregory was restlessly and impatiently in league with the stones of the field, and he had the highest expectations of his wholly unskilled labourer.

'Now, don't be making a hames of it,' he'd say caustically, as we built a perilous mountain of hay into the high-sided cart. In the evening, over supper, he'd mock my efforts to his sister or his mother, and we'd all laugh. They were exhausting days, making the best of the fair weather. Once the hay was mowed and turned, they raked it into cocks, or into stacks called trams, in bigger fields (such as those others owned on the plain of Kilmurvey), to keep it dry. Then the cocks or trams were broken up and the hay lugged to the cart, in ropes. Gregory had scarce a field into which he could drive a cart. You had a length of rope which you laid down in a long 'n'. Then you pitchforked hay across it, until you had as big a heap as you thought you could loop up in the rope and bear on your back. The rope cut hard into your shoulders and your hands. The geography of the fields meant you might have to go through several of them, through tight gaps, or down narrow paths between high walls, to the nearest point of access for the cart, and the ground was rough and rocky everywhere, up and down.

It was tough work, all day once the dew had lifted, in the heat, and a great struggle to keep the mound on your back from leak-ing, or toppling, bringing you down with it, especially if you got your instep snared by a bramble or your toe stubbed a rock. It felt almost like being in Lilliput, the way every thread of grass that could be saved was saved. When it came to rye, they reaped it, all but stem-by-stem with a little sickle. What Burns called a dai-mon icker in a thraive – a mouse's ration – was no small request on Aran. Not a grain was left, no luxury of gleanings here. And the rye, carried as the hay, was as slippery as eels, and almost impossible to cart when green, as it was when Gregory cut it to feed to his cattle.

It was amazing to work in this way, as primitive as anything in Europe, right at the edge of the western world, in a northern sea, like living in the corner of a scene by Bruegel. You could not guess how physically hard these men were, late and early, dawn to dusk, as certainly Gregory was, whose twin gods were work and land, land and work. I used to be put up to ride home on the high stack, steering the horse on a long rein, the cart rocking and grating through the narrow lanes, while Gregory and Bartley stepped out on either side, watching the empty road ahead, checking the ropes, helping us navigate the dangerous uphill corners where the load might slip and overturn the cart even. The sweet heat of the hay, soporific and intoxicating in limb and lung, made it the harder to slip down again at the end of the journey and begin once more to recycle every blade and stalk, forking it into the store. There were lulls during the day, when one task or another, weaning calves, watering the horse, milking the cow, intervened.

It was during such a lull, and at Mrs Feaney's suggestion, that I began to clip the privet hedge at the front of the house. By now the island was really filling up with tourists and the Feaneys' place aswarming. (I'd have my own guests too, a pair of schoolteacher friends from Liverpool to divert me for some happy days.) Mrs Feaney wanted to keep things smart, to make a good impression on new arrivals off the boat. I clipped up to one side of the gate before tea and then left the shears stuck upright in the hedgetop. But when I came back to complete the job, I found the shears gone. Gregory had confiscated them and left the job unfinished. Mrs Feaney flustered and flanneled, telling me not to worry. For his part, Gregory would say nothing. But for an obscure reason, he was in a taking and would not have me trim the hedge, for all the world to see, I supposed, at the Dublin end of things – an odd suburban kind of inhibition? Or was I making a hames of it? I couldn't work him out at all and nearly gave up trying, as we finished the hay harvest and life slid back into its old pattern, fishing, scribbling, fishing, reading. But then a couple of evenings later, Gregory and his brother called me to the door. Would I like to come and help them with the Grey Fella?

# The Grey Fella and the Rocky Road

The Grey Fella was no pale horse. He was the finest, flintiest, limestone-enriched, charcoal-dappled animal you ever met on the road, coming at a trot on a halter, showing his paces at Galway fair. Will modern Ireland at last be born when you no longer see such a sight on the road? Men wheeling horses round in the street? Men with enough dung on their boots to plant an Aran field, as the old man wrote on his return in wonder at scenes, as he considered, a hundred or two hundred years behind the times?

I do not know when Gregory bought the Grey Fella, whether a hundred or two hundred years before, but he had kept him down through the winter in one of his more high-walled pocket meadows. Once I saw them clatter bareback to a springing halt at the head of the hill into the village, about eight of a wet, silvery January morning. The Grey Fella frisked against the rein, his neck sprung; his forefeet pranced paces on the spot, and he sprang on his haunches, hard to halt. While Gregory in his peaked cap, with a dewdrop on his nose (noted carefully in my journal), sat straight-backed and easy, legs dangling, before they sidled and stamped and sped off crabwise on their way again, to some other new, secluded pasture. You'd not see a better bareback seat on a horse anywhere on earth, from the outback of Connacht to Outer Mongolia.

'Yon fella,' Gregory observed later, when I asked after the horse, 'yon fella's as jumpy as a kangaroo with two tails.'

And then I never saw the horse again anywhere under the Atlantic sky. He had been like an apparition, a stunning grey horse among the grey rocks, barely broken to a rider. Gregory had already introduced the Grey Fella to the straddle, letting him feel the weight of it across his back and the band under his belly just as he'd have to feel the cart saddle. He'd worked him a few hours bearing panniers of sand up from the bay, in the late evening. Now he and his brother were to set about breaking him to the shafts of a flat barrow and to the road. They were at my door, calling from the road. So out I shot and got myself up on the tail of the barrow, legs hanging down, and hands gripping hard, with instructions to jump down if there was any trouble and get round to the horse's head if I could. So we teetered down on the unsprung barrow, with many falterings and expressions of doubt on the part of the Grey Fella, and much verbal coaxing and sucking of teeth, to say nothing of grinding rims down to the bay, and jolts up the spine, and jerks of the neck and wrists, stop-go, go-stop, slip and slide, now Bartley leading him by the bridle, then all of us off, and all of us aboard a few yards, until we reached the low road past the bay, where the running sea alarmed him and the light in the dune grass unnerved him, put the fear of God into him, made him 'as scared as a grasshopper' as it says in the Bible.

But on the old low road, an unmade road in those days, he settled a while and we ran a few hundred yards, swallowing the ground like charioteers, dauntless as if to meet armed men, until his ears sleeked back at something and nothing, and he brought us up in a sudden skidding halt, nostrils flaring, as he pawed the ground and reared and pawed the air and backed us round into the ditch and wall. Gregory stayed on board, standing, extraordinarily, to draw rein, while hooves stamped round us. I hung on to whatever of the rein and harness I could grab and lay back against them, hanging on my heels. Bartley struggled to get his fingers under the curb chain, under the mouth, to tighten the bit and bring the head down. And off we went again, walking most of the way at the horse's head, taking turns to ride on the fore-end or the tail-board, straggling along like a trio of tinkers under the darkening sky, all the footsore way at last to Kilronan. There we stopped in a lane below McDonough's, a highly orderly house, I should say, for the real object of the exercise, two or three pints each, in rotation: one attending the Grey Fella while the other two drank.

I'd once nearly died on a wild red horse called Fox when I was a nine-year-old. I landed on my head on the hard metalled road after he'd bolted for a quarter of a mile or more. I missed most of a term of school in consequence, which was the silver lining, the lucky horseshoe up the devil's sleeve. Who knows but the concussion improved me, the cloud of unknowing? Otherwise the incident taught me, in old Mrs Feaney's own words, never to trust a horse. So when the brothers left me, as casually as you like, to stand and hold the Grey Fella by rein and bridle, and pacify him, and keep him from scrambling his brains with head-tossing, or from kicking himself lame against the barrow, I had to forget Fox – the red horse, mythical sign of strength and virility, whose tearaway hooves still rang in my memory – and concentrate on the grey, the horse of death, and let him not be the death of me. But as the light faded, the Grey Fella settled, and so did I.

The crack I had with Bartley and Gregory by turns ran upon horses, nothing but horses. Bartley would talk about horses every hour of the day. Not just the virile Fox amused him but another red horse in the field, the Capall Mór, did I remember? I remembered very well. That was the big horse, red as you like, ridden to victory that year on the holiday for Saints Peter and Paul at the end of June, by a slip of a red-haired boy. He was not much older than I had been when Fox threw me. But he was a thousand-thousand times the better horseman, the butcher's son from Oatquarter. In the weeks and days to the end of the month, the red-haired boy had been coming down to the strand at Kilmurvey to canter his mount in the surf and have it toughen its hooves and hocks, its knees and fetlocks, in the brine. It was a stirring sight on a bright evening with far-away Connemara for hazy backdrop, the courageous bareback rider, as old as time.

I knew his family only because I regularly bought meat from them. His sister used sometimes to bring it, on Saturday mornings. She was a very pretty little girl with long chestnut hair, all freckles like her brother. Once a friend sent me in the post an article about Aran from an American photo-journalistic magazine. It had a big double-spread in it of this child whirling round in the schoolyard, her hair flying, dancing right at the centre of the shot. I made a gift of it to her the next time she brought the meat and you'd have thought I'd given her the world twice over. We're not supposed to love our own image but there are ages when we do, when we may be rapt by the sight of ourselves. And why not? A little narcissism is no dangerous thing. Would the same could be said for knowledge. So I had chatted with her brother, now and then, if we met on the strand, to talk about the horse and the event ahead, the race on the sands in Killeany Bay (Aran's answer to the Laytown meeting), for which he was preparing. The main part of his preparation, it seemed, was to gallop up off the strand and onto the metalled road, uphill all the way to Oatquarter, a scary ride bareback on such a big horse. For the Capel Mor was indeed, as his name indicates, a big horse; and the red-haired boy not yet a youth, yet somehow he seemed twice that and more, an old head on young shoulders.

'He does be too strong for me,' the boy would assure me, trying to rein him in while we talked. 'I cannot stop him when he has his head.'

When I asked him if he was afraid, his answer came plain and unhesitating, with the broadest grin.

'I am scared. You know? By Christ I am.'

I knew, I tried to tell him, but then he was off, no choice in the matter, heading for the edge of the dune and the road.

'Will you win the race?' I called up to him the next time.

'I will not,' he laughed back, 'or I will, if ever he will take the corners. If I can turn his head, I will win, for there's no other horse has his legs.'

And of course he won, champion of the Western World, against a mixed field, including a menagerie of also-rans, sporting misfits, winkered mules, and made everyone's day that beautiful low-tide morning, if no one's fortune, galloping with grace round the ribbed and plashy shore, on a triangular course marked out by curragh sticks stuck in the sand, taking those corners wide, in an easy, seamless stride (a race a bit like this sentence). That was the day of the races: horse races, bicycle races (round a little humpy field), curragh races (six-oar, and eight-oar, with competitors from the islands), the Pan-Aran Games you might call them, the Galway Bay Olympics.

We came back that night on the high road in the all-but-dark halfmoonlight, with hardly a faltering step or a dismount. And so we went the next night and the next night, and then just Gregory and I went and came cartwheeling home, later and later, hunched up, clipping along, all full of talk and Guinness, talk about how well the Grey Fella was coming on, about the Missus.

'And you wanted us to think you had a wife,' he threw in finally one night, laughing at me, as at the fool of men.

'Well …'

'Wasn't that funny, now? and she was only your girlfriend,' he mocked.

So, as I had guessed, the ghost of Christy's father had tided it over, and it was thought a great joke, and its confession made an opening for Gregory and for me, in a strange and pleasant way, to regard each other on an easier, jocular footing. Not that Gregory was less hectic and intense than before, not that he was so much more forthcoming.

Those days were somehow contrapuntal. In the one direction ran the tide of tourists (and of my own two guests in August), and visitors of all kinds who came to my door – miscellaneous poets, journalists, Yanks, Bretons, to hear my story, as if it were over, which made me feel ambivalent towards them: I didn't want to be drawn into their world. They had no idea what times I'd had, through November and December, January, February and March – how I'd served my time, on the bare floor of my hearth, the long nights of solitude, the rattling storm-bound days, the empty days on the bare rock, days when you said aloud more to yourself than to any other living soul. On entirely another scale, in a different rhythm, there was my daily life, fishing, beachcombing, making do, running the Grey Fella down to Kilronan with Gregory and coming back drunk. That was the life that seemed most real, if it wasn't for the clock ticking louder and louder against me, the days already shorter.

I spent one memorable evening with my Liverpudlian guests in Conneely's American Bar. Kilronan in those days was already far more modern than the wilds to the west, where we had no electricity, and life was scarcely altered by technology. Some of us had tap-water in those days, others didn't. But that's hardly technology, a standing tap. No one had the telephone, except in Kilmurvey at the guesthouse cum post-office. I'd see people in Kilronan, especially now in the summer, who didn't know me from Adam, people who weren't quite sure who I was. I certainly didn't seem like a visitor, and yet? They could be rough places to be in the winter months, some of those Aran bars. In the summer, as I say, they opened up a little. But not that much. There were still fights and violences.

'Dig your grave,' mad Dara from Killeany would challenge the hook-nosed Connacht Spaniard, Marcus, 'Dig your grave', squaring up again for the hundredth time. I saw them one Saturday night outside the village hall, the cock of the east versus the cock of the west, posturing. Marcus, I noted, looked 'white and drawn', tensing for it, as his friends held him back, and he made out to resist them, with occasional shrugs and lunges, feints in a ritual. Everyone said Dara was afraid of no one and no thing. One time at least he slipped undetected aboard the *Naomh Eanna* and, as she crossed the bar, dived off the stern to swim back to Kilronan in the icy tide. So one man assured me. This time the scrap was broken up by a priest before it began, and spectators dispersed, disappointed, not caring to admit tbat the ritual was the thing nine cases out of ten. You've seen the kind of display in the schoolyard yourself. There was many a more serious squabble and many a lesser one to witness week by week. That early evening late in August my guests and I were drinking in Conneely's, with a handful of locals and a handful of tourists. Someone started to sing, 'I'm a wandering tinker, I've travelled my share / And I've courted the colleens from Antrim to Clare ...' And then others were called upon to sing, until singing suddenly became compulsory.

'You must contribute, or you cannot leave,' one of the locals declared, vehemently, as another went to bar the door.

'You must contribute ...'

An old man, drunk to the skies (a man I'd encountered on the road one night early in my stay), had begun now to engage my friends with a story. It was a dramatic story, a tragic story, that he'd obviously recounted many times before. He couldn't dramatize it enough, so he over-dramatized it. (But we artless autobiographers should shtick together.)

'Three days and nights with a dead man in a curragh, until we were washed up on the shores of County Clare,' he kept saying, grasping my friend by the sleeve, staring round into his face with a solicitous stare, 'three days and nights, with a dead man in a curragh'.

You had to see them limping to rescue one of their number after the curragh had wallowed and shipped the worst part of a wave and been righted. You had to think of the desperation, struggling half-drowned themselves, in the dark cold and storm-chopped sea, darkness on the face of the deep, to direct the curragh, with just three sticks now, towards their struggling comrade as he went down, and surfaced, calling, his voice faint on the wind and roar, and down, until entirely by luck they got to him, and he was dragged inboard to gasp his last. You had to see the way the storm gathered with the night, and how they drifted helpless, slung between peaks, swung up out of troughs, and the long day ahead, and the night, and the day again, without rescue, the seas impossible, as rigor mortis set in. 'Three days and nights ...'

The old man sang a song in Irish, holding out his hands on either side for those beside him to pump the song out of him (as if pumping water from a sinking vessel). Someone sang 'The Croppy Boy'.

'Come on, now,' the locals menaced the visitors, 'you must contribute, you must contribute ...'

I was leaning at the bar, ordering a round, and thinking quite light-heartedly to myself that on no account was I going to be bullied into 'contributing' anything for anyone. I set my face against it. If necessary, they could go to hell.

A Swede or Norwegian or maybe a German stood up to sing, sweating with anxiety, some queer yodelling thing, exposing the rest to greater pressure. Now my friend, betrayed, broke ranks and sang an English hymn. (Women, it seemed, were exempt.) What was it he sang? I can still see his nervous, schoolmaster's, honest Adam's apple wobbling as he warbled. But what did he sing? 'O God, our strength in ages past'? It was something anyway from the school's morning assembly, something as upright English as you could get. Shortly after my friend had finished, I decided we would leave and go on our way. So we drank up and rose to go and I stepped straight up to the fellow at the door. No matter what, I wasn't going to be stopped, and I wasn't going to sing. It might have been reckless. There had been at least one serious fracas recently. (There would be another before long.) Not that they'd singled me out. Not that they'd demanded a contribution from me. However it was, the fellow on the door didn't hesitate but stood aside, and off I went, puzzled. (I was no kind of physical threat to him.) I thought he perhaps took me for a native and was only out to make the tourists feel unwelcome. (A reasonable enough motive, you may think.) Maybe he was a MacCalor and knew my connections? But did I believe any of that? If I didn't believe it then, I would soon enough come to do so.

Time raced away now. The world seemed even to be changing. Those douce dulse days were numbered.

It was Mary who came, excitedly, all the way from the post office.

'A man on the line, ringing from Fleet Street, for you. He says he'll wait …'

A momentous event, it was indeed, and for me as unreal as a phone call from Mars might be. I closed myself into the small booth, next to the groceries, aware I was probably being eavesdropped at the switchboard, and heard for the first time about events in the North. Did I know there'd been riots on the streets of Belfast and Londonderry? (London-derry as he put it, in that same ruling accent that would later ooze so resonantly and resolutely, insensitive to its own history, from the lips of Whitelaw and Mayhew.)

'What do the people on the island think?'

'News travels slow,' I said, 'I haven't heard. I don't know ...'

All that world of telegrams and anger was far behind me now. I would not return to it. But I thanked my friend for being in touch and said goodbye and set out back for home. What did the people think, enveloped there? I couldn't say. What did I think? What rough beast was it that now slouched along the road to be reborn? It was too remote and too early in the day to read any such writing on the wall from where I stood. Life on the island went on as if nothing had happened in the great world. There were more pressing things at hand to think about.


'They're exploring,' said Gregory, pushing his cap off his brow to see.

We were harnessing the Grey Fella and had stopped to watch the light plane, belated sign of the modern world, that had come combing up the evening sky, low along the Atlantic shore, circling, and looping, and running back on itself, reconnoitring, a pathfinder, faintly sinister. We'd all seen it before, in the past few days, making its long runs in and out. They were surveying, the word was, for the coming airstrips, and that was suddenly all the talk. An age was about to end. History was rapidly completing its metamorphosis into heritage. There would soon be airstrips on the islands, no more sea-governed isolation, no more shortages, fewer dire emergencies; and a hotel to be built, they rumoured, a monstrous invasion at Kilmurvey bay. Could it be? So much the better, it might seem to most, long overdue.

Gregory and I nowadays almost rocketed down the low road to Kilronan, as if behind Pegasus. The Grey Fella hardly needed by this time more than a little coaxing to breast the air round the bay and to trot with scarce a whinny or a shy beyond the whistling shimmer of the dunes. On one of the last such trips we made, before I said goodbye and hit the road to Dublin, Gregory seemed in an especially manic mood. We left early and were supposed not to be late back, because he hadn't milked the cow, and he had to milk the cow because at the last Mary had refused. Instead of taking turns to take a pint we left the Grey Fella to it and drank the more, maundering over our drinks about the approaching winter. I because I was leaving, to do what? I didn't know. Gregory because it was almost winter again and because, now, anyway, we must get back to milk the cow. So we flew back on the high road, recklessly boneshaking it along as far as the hill at Oatquarter where we had to slow to the usual lurching, slipping, clopping pace, round the smithy corner and onto the long hill. We'd had enough to drink for me to suggest we could do worse than stop in at Dirrane's for one more. One more for the road.

Once, on the feast of Glorious Mary in the middle of August (the anniversary of the great disaster of 1852), when a crowd of Inishmaanites came over and travelled out to the Feaneys' house and there was drink and music, and the old crone Maggie Faherty danced in the lane, they had sent me up to Dirrane's for 'a crate of drink'. I'd have to go alone, and so too I'd have to struggle back with it alone, a dozen pint bottles in a crate. No one else would come and no one explained why they wouldn't but Mrs Feaney fussed over it and gave me the money. When I got there they were closed, which was unusual, but at my repeated knocking the landlady came to the door. She looked at me askance. In the end I had to plead with her to serve me.

It wasn't ever my favourite venue, as you know. But I was oiled enough not to care too much about that, the night Gregory and I came home to milk the cow. He didn't reply to my suggestion but as we approached the entrance up to the pub he drew rein and brought us to a halt in the middle of the road.

'You can go in if you want,' he said, flatly, 'and I will go on. It's late now. The cow will burst asunder if I stop now, anyway.'

In that case, I said I wasn't interested and we resumed our way, hooves slipping and sliding on the tarmac and overhead the wind keening in the telephone wires, its unforgettable wilderness elegy, as the stars pricked sharper and sharper holes in the night.

'The truth is,' Gregory confessed, 'I am barred from Dirrane's, d'you see?'

Hot-tempered I knew him to be but never a brawler, surely to God he never was? And never the kind of fool I had been? I was surprised, and then not so surprised, for I knew too well how anything could happen in an Aran bar when the bachelors got cranky.

'It is a long story,' he said at last, weighing up whether to let me in on it any further, and seeming to decide not to.

Or, if he meant to begin, before he could do so we were down on the crescent road, the sea was pounding in the bay and the Grey Fella, with home in his nostrils, was ripping along as if the cart was made of matchwood. We couldn't hear each other speak. By the time we'd rubbed the horse down, put away the harness and cart, led him to his grazing, scrambled after the cow and got her – she was in a mood – to behave well enough to give the milk that otherwise she was so anxious to give ('like a bladder fit to burst', said Gregory), neither of us approaching sober, we'd missed the moment for his story and I had to wait to pursue it next day. And this is how I scribbled it in my journal:

*We didn't go to Kilronan because of the torrential rain. But I was in this evening, talking to Gregory and Mary and Mrs Feaney. Mrs Feaney went off in her scarf to see a neighbour and so I asked Gregory right out, how was it he came to be barred from Dirrane's? Why wouldn't he tell me? It had amused me to hear it, given my own experiences there. I tried to coax it out of him by telling him I was less than welcome there myself and how I never chose to drink there now. 'Don't be telling me. You think I don't know?' he laughed. Mary began to encourage him, in Irish, at least it sounded like encouragement, in that clipped sideways way Mary has of showing her less caustic side. But he didn't mind telling me, he said. 'A few weeks, a month anyway, before you came to Aran,' he began, 'in the month of September, my brother Anthony was home from Boston after – how many years would it be since we last clapped eyes on the bugger? ... too many to count. Anyway, now he was leaving again and we were at Dirrane's with a few fellas. And there was an argument about a bicycle that was stolen from us by one of the O'——s. Then Anthony stuck a couple of clatters on one of them, and they did bar me. They accused me of putting him up to it, like. So I am barred.' But that wasn't the half of it, said Mary, so. Would he tell me or would she? So between them they told me how on the day Anthony sailed they'd had a party at the house. They were all 'kind of merry', you know, and sad in their hearts at once, on account of Anthony and how they'd maybe never see him again. You know. And Gregory and Bartley had gone with him to the steamer. And Mary sat in the kitchen with her mother weeping and playing records on the gramophone, with the door open, jigs and reels and airs, John McCormack. And the house seemed so empty, with the door open, and their hearts were empty, because it is a very hard thing to say goodbye to a son and brother. And Gregory came home at last, with Bartley, drunk, the way he was talking, anyway. Mary laughed. And they nagged Bartley to get away out of it to see his missus, and Gregory to milk the cow. And he went off muttering, as usual, cursing them. Then as he came round a corner in one of the narrow tracks where the stone walls are too high to see over, three O'—— brothers jumped him and battered the lights out of him, in payment with interest for Anthony's work at Dirrane's.*

This terrible incident was part of a tribal vendetta that went back farther than anyone could properly remember. Affected by it, I made an even cruder version in my journal of the crude verses below (which allude, impertinently, to the drunken image at the close of Richard Murphy's very beautiful poem called 'Sailing to an Island' – any more ugly and worse than which this one could hardly be):

SAILING FROM AN ISLAND

All summer the Atlantic boomed and idled.
The tourists came, were conquered, and set sail,
wearing new bonnets and sweaters
and a happy tourist smile.

Poets among them wrote their poems
in terse vocabulary of ocean gales
and stone and light and some-or-other
fishing-bird or -boat, or saint,
metaphors for their art's endurance.

The clock ticked by the china cock.
John McCormack whined and crackled
his past tense at the open door.
The cooker creaked and steamed
beneath a blessed trinity
of Pope and Christ and Kennedy.
Bottles stood empty on the table.
His sister cried and struggled not to.
He dreamed the dream of exile and escape.

His brother Anthony the Yank
had sailed that evening's autumn tide
Boston-bound and in his wake
bequeathed to him a reignited feud
with the tribe they dubbed 'The Twenties':
his parting shot 'a couple of clatters'
stuck hard on one of them,
refuelling their landwar hate
over the ownership of a bike.

Outside the failing evening wavered
like a candle in a draught.
The ocean filled a conch with sound

> while three waited in the boreen for him
> to beat his head full and empty
> of stars, that woke his swollen gaze,
> spinning and burning overhead,
> as he stared up among the stones.

My last days and hours on Aran are almost unbearable even now to try to write about, the dream weighted with realism for proper ballast, but still the haunted and haunting dream of sea-wilderness and poignant hardship rising up. How goodbye is just two abrupt syllables, a shake of the hand and you must turn and go at last, abruptly as you came, a freakish visitor, back into your past. What was everything, through thick and thin, is suddenly nothing but the stuff of stories, like your childhood, like a documentary-movie dream, like the Ancient Mariner's inscrutable distress, like Gulliver coming back to talk to the horses, like an obituary notice. You say your farewells for ever after. You've no home to go to until you've left it far behind. You remember and you misremember. You keep it too yourself, like five minutes' wisdom. You emulate the *omertà* of the old men from the sea. They're leaning on their elbows on the wall, staring at an empty horizon, smoking their silver-capped pipes, spitting at their boots, minds blank. But the slightest encouragement and you spill your all, to whomever will listen again, if only out of politeness. You celebrate the time you rebelled and kicked against the pricks, and caution others against it, against romantic folly, against transcendental self-indulgence, when at heart you wonder what else is there to recommend? Of all the responsible, dutiful courses, what? Beyond parenting, that intimate Shakespearean verity, what? (The O'Hamlets, Macbeths, and crazy O'Lears on the wilderness heath?) What? In God's name what? The good republic? I drink and pray to the founding of the good republic. The republic where a man's a man for a' that, and a' that, and a woman a woman.

It was a Galway Fair sailing and Gregory and Bartley had cattle to sell. So they had hit the drovers' road early that morning before the day was light and it was Colm who drove me to Kilronan in his van. By eight-fifteen − who goes there? − we were knocking on the door at Kenny's bar, to find the place roaring full, as if Tam O'Shanter had forgotten to go home the night before. This was a revelation to me, after hours drinking before hours ('I never saw him drunk but then again I never saw him sober, if you get my meaning,' as the man said), burning the candle at both ends. It was here I was introduced by Colm to the prisoner, who shall be nameless, the prisoner at the bar, you might say. Dressed in his Sunday best, but shirt open at the neck, the prisoner − in his DA haircut, Brylcreemed (redhead), spick and span, white socks, best black winkle-pickers, raw red labourer's hands (too big, you'd think, to get down his blue sleeves) − was bailed to see the magistrates that week, or day was it?, on a charge of one degree or other of bodily harm, actual or grievous, I'll let the lawyers among you take your pick. He had cut someone's face open with a broken glass in a drunken brawl just a few nights before, and I was to aid and abet his escape. Everyone in Kenny's conspired at it, by paying us no attention, but passing round drinks. Guinness for breakfast. Everyone on the island conspired at it, as far as I could make out, including the victim and the guard, if not the priest or the magistrate, and I was the perfect cover. No one on Aran, it seemed to me, had much sympathy for law enforcement, they preferred the people's anarchy. They preferred to forgive for the moment, and remember for the future, as Gregory knew. Colm's plan was that I would take the prisoner's suitcase aboard with my baggage. As there was such a consensus gathered, I drank my payment and agreed. In this way, dear reader, I became an honorary member of the Irish criminal classes, still wanted to this day, I'm sure.

They were busy with the cattle on the quay, winching them into the hold in the sling. The man who owned the big fields at Kilmurvey also owned a bull that he was now to sell, and the bull was down there, and all the men – Gregory and Bartley among them – were managing it. When all the stock were in the ark, Gregory drew me aside, not so much to say a last goodbye as to tell me his distress. He'd been down that morning on his land beyond Portmurvey and found whole strips of wall laid low, the sides of two fields and more, all toppled to the ground. It was a continuation of the feud by the O'——s.

'That bastard,' he said, naming the one in particular that his brother the Yank had clattered.

So we said goodbye, in some agitation. And Colm helped me get my bags and my excess baggage aboard, while the prisoner took a turn up and down the quay, as inconspicuous as if he were in evening dress and smoking a cigar. The guard was down there, looking away. They withdrew the gangway. They cast off for'ard. The *Noamh Eanna* began just to swing out. They were next to cast off aft and as they prepared to, the prisoner skipped out from among the men and hopped aboard, brazen as you like, as nimble as if he did it for a living. The only thing the performance lacked was a round of applause. I nodded at him as he ducked out of sight, into the saloon, and I went to stand to the last at the stern as we began the long sorry run back via the islands, until I could see Inishmore no more – finishmore, the end only begun, as the islands sank away. I went to find the prisoner to be sure he knew where his suitcase was and he thanked me again and bought me a drink. And there I stood drinking in the press of folk, with the tourists and islanders in the saloon, drinking to forget (the whole episode behind me), as the *Naomh Eanna* throbbed down the bay, at speed with the weather behind her.

By the strangest chance, some American youths beside me began, amid much laughter, to tell the others they were with how drunk they'd been the night before. They'd got so wildly destroyed, in fact, that they'd tried to find their way home through some fields. In the effort they toppled a bit of a wall. Being far gone, they then set to and knocked down the whole wall, and they had a go at another one for fun, and … I couldn't believe my ears. I had to do something about it, to save Gregory from himself. I edged my way through to Bartley (travelling in for the next day's fair) and whispered in his ear what I'd heard, and by this accident prevented poor Gregory's paranoia getting the better of him. (I begged Bartley not to take it out on the youths, as he and his friends at first thought to do. He wasn't happy, but happier to know for his brother's sake.) Then, at last ashore in Galway, I took my leave of Bartley, and the prisoner, and, through his brother, my last leave of Gregory too, who had nursed what driven griefs of mind all through my stay, out in the savage wilderness?

Next morning, the coda to my story goes, I was coming down

the steps from the Bank of Ireland, having withdrawn enough money to see me down the road to Dublin, then to Holyhead (wished meself was dead), and on to see the boys of Liverpool (called meself a fool). As I reached the bottom step, I became aware of someone calling after me. I looked round, and there was the cashier, in his shirtsleeves, agitated, waving a slip of paper. I remember seeing him in slow-motion and registering the patches of sweat in his armpits as he waved and flapped, breathless, that mild late autumn day. Should I take a leaf out of the prisoner's book or should I wait to discover by how much I was overdrawn? It was no comfort to think it metaphorically fitting to find myself without credit in the world.

## Postscript: Aran 2000

The truth is, you can't return anywhere. When and to what might you do so? In what precise moment? Even a place as threadbare as Inishmore changes. The laws of economics necessitate it. Here's a once inconceivable minibus abandoned and rusting to nothing on the rocks. Its windows out and wheels off, it looks otherwise as if headed to eternity on a crazy outing, a drinking spree perhaps, without an engine. There's another facing the opposite way, FERRY LINK SHUTTLE BUS, going nowhere. People die. Dynasties lapse. O'Kosan v. MacCalor: what's the score? Who's winning now? Go round the graveyards at Kilmurvey and Killeany and see for yourself.* Buildings are abandoned and fall into ruin. The smithy at Oatquarter first to go? Conneely's guesthouse at Kilmurvey next? With its windows boarded

---

*See too how on the island English remains the preferred language of epitaph. Perhaps because it's cheaper to carve than Irish? Or maybe because it sets death apart?

up, it shocks the eye to see it, whether or not you knew it thirty years ago. Then it was the mid-island hub, lit up at night like a luxury liner, to steer you home through the rip tides of Guinness. What story stands behind its ruin, its plot drawn from a Greek tragedy? How terribly the world can change. No wonder the driver ignored me when I asked to go there and took me to stay elsewhere instead. New buildings rise, new bungalows especially. There's ribbon development at Oatquarter, urban sprawl at Onaght. Even the coffin they carry you off in enjoys, it seems, a new lease of life. That old Irish institution is an especially potent totem in the symbology of Aran, as witness its supporting role in Synge's *Riders to the Sea*. Now, as I overheard on my visit, the latest drama has men taking a body out of one and replacing it with drugs, in a sleight-of-hand passage, in and out of Inishmaan (location of Synge's famous play). Imagine the scene: Enter McCox and O'Box, with dope and a corpse, and the cops in pursuit, out in that most desolate stony place at the edge of the Atlantic. The laws of nature dictate their game too. Weeds well up in the gardens. Land's set aside. History converts into heritage. Visitors are offered a 'Culture Week' away. How could Inishmore escape, and why should it? Materially these are better times for the people who remain, though the young still look to leave.

'Everything has changed,' said Michael Gill's son Patrick, 'but what has changed everything most is television, working behind the scenes.'

It was electricity that made the difference. A thing we did not have. It would take more than the occasional power cut to let you see just what that means, minute by minute, night and day, week upon week, through every season. Now as the Internet vies with the fishing net, tourists in ever-greater droves (their first port of call an Aran portal on the World Wide Web?) come with their money to see what is no longer to be seen, except in museums, with sound effects of the sea, trailing *Man of Aran*. While outside on the quayside and the harbour road the jarvies hustle from their minibuses, as if in Kingston or Havana, waving their maps in one hand, gesticulating, and smiling their smiles, pointing to the usual tourist hotspots with a stabbing finger, tracing a rapid route round, for a few punts, as the visitors troop by. Though the rocks and the sea outlast it all, as dramatic to the eye as ever, and as always there's the island weather, its infinite variations of light and sea and rain and stone. Unless, that is, global warming should prove to be the undoing of us all, and the sea rise to reign once more through aeons of new geology.

It's not true to say that the only returning you ever do is in the mind. But in that sense I was back there time and again, every day, as a hedge against the times. To go there in my head like that, as I still do now and then in wonder at the place, delivers an emotional charge, strangely compounded of longing and of loss, bittersweet to darken my gain. All my gain being what this book amounts to, and the heart's catchment from which it's drained? As you sow so shall you reap. The least loaded way of putting it seems to be to say, I went there a third time. But of course my going was loaded to the gunwales with my story. That was in May (now it's early September, as I tweak this essay, and I'm on my way back from Inishmore again). As when I first went, people now wondered, as I also wondered, should I go? Wouldn't I be disappointed? But if I would be disappointed surely I'd deserve to be? Or had I learnt nothing since November 1968? It wasn't that I thought the gardaí would want to question me regarding the prisoner, although his name may be on the books still, charges not answered, after all these years. He might be scot free in Kilburn or California, for all I know. I just decided I'd go unannounced and incognito, for amusement, out of curiosity, and perhaps a little caution. Keep your name to yourself, I urged myself. Play the strategist for once. Just a word told under such circumstances will be a truth at least, about the playboy. Did you ever know a young fellow-my-lad lived here once, in 1968-69? (I didn't.) Not that I hadn't been in touch in all that time. I'd had a little correspondence. But replies could take a long time coming. One letter I sent waited three years for an answer. In which time I feared the worst. But I mostly knew before I landed who had died since my time. I learnt late of Mikey McDonough's tragic drowning, by a chance encounter with Padraig O'Cleary of the Gaelic League, coming over on the Dublin–Galway train. Lost at sea. (What terrible words to breathe. Though no man at all can be living forever.)

When Odysseus went again to Ithaca he was aided there in his subterfuges by Pallas Athene. No great strategist myself, as you know, I can yet say I was aided by a deity too. But this was another class of being, if one no less powerful: the obscurer goddess Amnesia. You recall? No one knew who I was. (So if you include me that made all of us.) My sojourn had been as a sparrow's flight through the great hall, as the Venerable Bede said. It meant everything to me but to the people of Kil-na-cer it flew by very quickly, as fleeting as the hour scarce heeded. Having come out of the winter, it soon returned to winter, and slipped out of sight, and out of mind. I had to introduce myself by stages but even then things seemed to hold together only briefly, before drifting apart again, like wreckage on the sea dispersing, like the bones of the drowned on the shifting seabed of North Sound. You see the world as you did when you were young. Nothing, it seems, will lastingly persuade you that the body your eyesight belongs to has grown older with the passing times. Though we know nothing to be more eternally true than that it has, even beyond recognition. I say no one knew me, but then only a handful had survived who could possibly have told who I was from Adam. Thirty years is a lifetime. The playboy had been in reality just a youth, a boy almost, and he'd had a head of hair. I was now balder and far burlier than ever he'd looked to become. You'd have to search my dial with unbecoming attention, eyes like a phrenologist's stout fingers, feeling out bumps of knowledge, to make me out for what I was before, so long ago. I was just a 'blow-in', a vagrant bird.

So I checked myself in at a place near Kilmurvey, lucky to be able to do so, without booking in advance, my old preference for chance still with me. I'd thought, as I say, that I'd stay at Conneely's but Conneely's was no more, these ten years since. Seeing in the living-room while I waited the picture of someone I recognized, I let the cat out of the bag straightaway. Then the first thing I did, and not without great trepidation, was to go through Kilmurvey and on up to Kil-na-cer to call on Gregory. Mary eventually welcomed me in. As I stood at the door – familiar door, Yale key in place to admit whoever might try (but I thought a little formality necessary now) – I heard what I took to be someone on a stick and had a sudden vision of Gregory as an old man. But it was poor Mary, recovering, as she told me, from an illness. I saw in her, I thought, the young woman I'd known, and also something more, it seemed, of her mother. Her memory wasn't good, poor soul, and she couldn't recall me.

'Ah, Gregory would remember,' she said. 'Gregory is away, you know, to see a man about some cattle, out in Gort na gCapall. He'll not be back much before six, I'd say.'

It sounded like the old days. We spoke about the dead, above all of a brother tragically lost.

'Such good fun, he was too. Such good fun,' she said.

('A gas man,' said Michael.)

Then I went exploring towards Gort na gCapall, half hoping to come upon Gregory while I stayed on the road. But I soon left the beaten track and quartered off whole acres of the island. Down towards Gort na gCapall I went and to the sea, to look again at Poll na bPeist, and back along the way to Blind Sound, reserving Dún Aengus for the morning. My mind reeled as I went, reeled and unreeled. I walked as if entranced, stepping in and out of time, up off the boreen and through the narrow ways between the fields of stone, hacking the briars with my stick. The blaze of the invisible Atlantic up ahead fired the evening sky and its din flew round me on the breeze. In an instant it was just more than thirty years ago. To my surprise, I even recognized individual rocks. I felt the familiar limpid light lighten my step, as if I'd re-become the playboy himself, crossing the karst where the sea-pinks blew and the shale rattled, where the rock looked like untarnished lead in the strong sea-light. You'd think the stone had been poured into place and just spilt over some mysterious mould. I looked in amazement at the terrible desolation, at the overhanging cliffs, at where I used to climb down to the point to fish, and died a thousand deaths to contemplate the risks, over the precipice from which I stood well back now, wobbling a nervous camera. What was it that was in me in those days?

There'd been such a sudden squall as we'd landed at Kilronan, aboard the *Draoicht na Farraige* (Magic of the Sea: built in Australia), it dispersed the minibus jarvies to their cabs and made the visitors huddle and hurry. But now, in one of those micro-climate switches so typical of the islands, the sky ran bright and blue, thinning slowly towards night. I wanted just to keep on walking, taking it all back in, to let everything fit together, like a jigsaw, the pieces I'd carried all these years with those of the present moment, then and now. So I went on, past the old well where Maggie Feaney took her pails, and past the new Dún Aengus heritage centre, where once stood Sonny Hernon's store, and the new An Sunda Caoch (Blind Sound) café and little tourist shops, and the seafood restaurant, and then on and up and round to Kil-na-cer, and past my own house, now so modernized it fairly broke my heart, and on again.

I couldn't walk enough. The evening was beginning just to fail. And then as I looked up from the road, I saw Gregory himself, riding down on a mountain bike, coming from the ball alley, behind his collie. I hailed him and he stopped. There was no mistaking him, all right, his back straight, his left eye just a little watery from the breeze and the bicycle. He searched my face for a clue. I could not believe how little he'd aged in appearance. He couldn't believe, it seemed, the things I appeared to know about him and the people of those days. He stood there astride his crossbar, puzzling. Then gradually, it seemed, he connected things together. But he couldn't recall the Grey Fella, in a long sequence of different horses down the years. So why would he remember me, who was so much less useful than a horse? So much lower than a Houyhnhnm? After so long, of course, there's everything and nothing to be said. We ran through the roll-call of the living and the dead, who'd married whom and what families they'd had. Who'd left for Connemara, who'd gone to Galway, who to America (half the world), and who'd returned. He still kept a pony, a pale horse, paler than the Grey Fella this time, and cattle the length and breadth of the place.

'You must be the richest man on Aran these days,' I said.

'Why would you be saying that now?' he smiled. 'Ah, sure,' he said, 'there's no money in cattle now. You're better off without them, like. Though prices do be better this year than anything these five years since, I'd say, anyway.'

I wondered would he let me buy him a drink before I went away. But he hadn't taken drink in six years. He was seventy-six, some twenty-three years my senior, as I never knew before. And so we said goodbye and I said I'd come to find him the next day. He was extremely polite and gracious, but still puzzled by me. My head swam to contemplate his life in that one place, for seventy-six years, with scarce a departure anywhere. A Zen-life, almost, a spiritual-material life so plain, so that when he died you knew he'd have to go instantly to the heaven he believed in. I felt second-rate beside him, with my questions, my assumption of familiarity.

By nightfall it was raining, fine rain on the wind, sea-rain ready-salted. But feeling as ever restless, and troubled at heart too, out I went to wander round and round, up and down, in my gentleman's Gore-Tex coat and over-trousers, and poking along with a stick, nightwalking, savouring the rain and the seaweed scents it released from the strand and shoreline. The sea was in everything. It was May and so I had my ears pricked for one thing only: to hear the corncrake, to plug in and recharge my nostalgia. But though now it was well past nightfall, not a one struck up its grating nocturne. I listened and listened. I stood still to silence my rustling waterproofs. I pulled off my hood to dampen the pricking noise of the rain. The more I listened, the greater and more overwhelming the silence I heard, the vaster the emptiness. The corncrake in its absence silenced the whole world. It stilled the Atlantic shore from here to Newfoundland, from here to Tierra del Fuego, from pole to pole. I was dismayed. Everything I had said before, earlier in these pages, about a world without them, had come true. The night was now incalculably small and dull, unadventurous, spring unsprung, the clock no longer ticking. Not a star in sight either, come to think of it. Not a crex, or a crex, but a more of crux or a crunch.

I learnt next day there had been no corncrakes on the island for at least ten years and more, maybe twenty (opinions differed). In local terms it seemed inexplicable. The people used no chemicals and no machinery on the land. In fact the land was richer than ever in flowers and grasses. More of it went the summer long untended, as never before. Perhaps it was the increased volume of traffic on the roads disturbing the environment? Or was it, as some said, that all those years back they'd started to cut the grass earlier in the season? That sounded like it to me. I tried to imagine the moment the last island corncrake took wing, at the end of a summer. I wondered how it could be that not a single one returned again, in whatever year it was they had first failed. Did one perhaps arrive and find himself alone, crexing to no challenge from another? The whole territory of Aran his oyster? Did he find it eerie and freak out? Did his heart falter and did he then pack his bags and sling his hook, before summer had a chance to show? Did he pass unknowing on his way another heading out down Galway Bay, a plump female?

As if to compensate, the cuckoos around Kilmurvey House that night went at it hammer and tongs. On they sang 'cuckoo' and louder sang, till ten and eleven o'clock, whirring and purring and wooing in the rain. I had never heard the cuckoo in such numbers and passion before, as I heard that night and saw in the course of my stay. Next day out at Bungowla, the aspect grey, the sea running bitter in the narrow Sound, the cuckoos, with their short wings and long tails, hunted over the walls and little fields in rapid short flight. They hawked through the air, perching abruptly on walls, before shooting away again. Once still they looked like stone, perfectly camouflaged. Then they sprang swiftly to their business, two of them with a pipit following, and a third suddenly sweeping in. What were they doing? Pairing? Luring the pipit away in some mesmeric ritual? They mesmerized me, for sure, as they flew round and round that wild rocky place, and called and called to each other, their commonplace double-stop cuck-oo, their treble-stop cuckoo-cuck, and more amorously intimate purring. Then they would emit what seemed an alarm call, more like the note of a wading bird. They were utterly beautiful, perching, poised with shoulders dropped, such beautiful shoulders and tails furling in courtship or some other territorial ritual. How absurd that we have requisitioned them for our petty fables of adultery. Will I mourn them too one day? When their hosts become extinct, if not before?*

Try as I might, I could not connect with Michael. I left a message with Katie, his wife. He left a message at my lodging. And my time now was running out, my dream up against the clock again. As I tried to hunt him out, I saw Gregory again, in the little field beside his house, cutting clumps of briars, methodically with a sickle, bending and shaping the thorns into cocks. He knew I was passing but he kept on working and I didn't presume to trouble him there, as he stooped, bent like a set square, back as flat as a board, in his cap and big buff gardening gloves (a sign of the times). Then we met again and he spoke of his philosophy of working all the time, while he could, always with something to do, but as if appealing to me for reassurance, so sweetly modest was he, as if I knew anything about how to live. He seemed palpably conscious that he lived on borrowed time. He would make work to do, he said.

'It is better than sitting and waiting.'

I wondered if nowadays he ever went in to the Galway cattle fair.

'I do,' he said, 'sometimes, like.'

Was he ever in the plane? I was conscious of the planes skimming in and out from Killeany, conscious of knowing a time when they had yet to become a twinkle in the horizon's eye. He was always in them if he chose to go to Galway.

*I note some of the birds I saw: heron, cormorant, razorbill, herring gull, fulmar, black-backed gull, black-headed gull, kittiwake, common tern, gannet, curlew, redshank, turnstone, dunlin, sand-piper, sea-pie, cuckoo, skylark, pipit (meadow and rock), stonechat, wheatear, goldfinch, robin, swallow, lapwing, chough, magpie, mute swan, moorhen, mallard, hooded crow, raven, jackdaw, sparrow hawk, rockdove, wren. (No corncrake: do you hear?)

'Seven minutes in the air,' he laughed, 'better than any sea-crossing, I'd say, all right. They were hard days before on the *Naomh Eanna* if you went on Monday for Tuesday, you'd have to stop over, like, till Thursday.'

I didn't fuss to say farewell. I said I'd be back in the autumn and hoped to see him.

'If we are living,' he said, 'please God.'

There were two especially wild men on Inishmore in my time. Bare-knuckle fighters, kings of their respective corners of their overgrown schoolyard, I'd feared them in a general kind of way, I must say, and one of them in particular. He seemed to fear no one, tall and rangy, wide-shouldered Hector and Achilles in one that he was. Only a fool didn't take care to step round him then, especially if he'd drink taken and his dander up, in those old fighting, feuding days. I know I was probably protected from him by my particular connections, at least enough to make him think twice. (I remember once, maybe on Pattern Day, standing at the bar in Kenny's with Gregory between me and the man, who was scowling round at me, leaning forward on his elbows at the counter, and Gregory telling him to stop and leave me alone.) But now we were surely both too old for that? I learnt anyway that this particular character was around and I was keen to meet him.

'But, oh,' said my informant, who knew him very well, better than most, being his wife, 'he is calmed down since, thank God.'

Calmed down or not, I meant to see him for auld lang syne. I'm not the least bit superstitious, no more than ever I was, but I knew I would see him, that same morning, as if by a seventh

sense. I knew I'd catch him on the road, as he drove from Bungowla to Kilronan. It was my last day in my lodgings. My room
being booked to someone else in advance of my arrival, I planned
to leave for Kilronan and stay my last night there. I wanted to
explore the world around Killeany, traditionally the poorest place
on the island ('But like your Harlems and your slums anywhere,
it's all been yuppified at Killeany,' as the curator at the Dún Aengus Heritage Centre said – himself an incomer now domiciled
there, a former priest, a scholar of the Celtic and romance languages). I wanted to cross to Dún Dúchathair. I wanted to stand
above Gregory's Sound. I wanted to clamber round to Glassin
Rock. I wanted to see the blowholes where the Atlantic sent its
spume up like a whale. They had put my bag on a bus and would
deliver it to Kilronan for me. So I walked with just my stick and
guessed that if I came out at the crossroad above the clochán and
walked quietly along in the sunny morning, my man must come
in his trap in good time. Sure enough, there he came in his white
wool bonnet, trotting along behind me, gradually catching me up.
I half turned when I heard the hooves, to check who it was, but
then paid him no heed until he was upon me.

I called to him by name, taking a step into the road, in a manner that in the old days he might have taken for a challenge
(though not a challenge from me: I was always a very quiet person but would take my risks out of curiosity, and liking, and
sometimes too much Guinness, in pursuit of observation, copy
for my story, as you know). He seemed more than happy anyway
to stop and give me a ride. So I climbed into the trap and off we
went at a dawdling trot. At once we began laughing at what a
wild, wild man he'd been. I said I'd feared him, which amused

him but also I think embarrassed him a little to hear me say so plainly. I think he'd have preferred it if I hadn't said it, but I did. He asked if I'd like to go by the low road, now itself a metalled road. I was pleased to. I wanted to travel it again, and to remember, as I told him, how we broke the Grey Fella in along it. We spoke again about him and his love of fighting, and his love of Guinness. He put his head down and pummelled the air before him, laughing. But it's no more black stuff now for him, doctor's orders, not at least until his world goes dark. He produced a postcard from his pocket as we rode along. It was one of those cards that offers four little views. There in one of them was his young self with his black Iberian curls, mending a fishing net. He tried to identify who owned the legs in the picture of men carrying a curragh in the black-beetle-blindfold traditional manner. Was one of them Brian Hernon? Who could say? He used the card as a prop in his entertainment of the tourists. He loved to have the visitors to talk to. But you'd wonder about some of them and their interest in walls and water tanks. He had a corporate umbrella in his trap, he laughed to show me, to keep them dry if it rained.

'There's a water tank, I do tell them, and some of them do love to be seeing the water tanks. There's another water tank, I say. That kind of way. But sure we're not interested in them. We see enough of them like,' he laughed, and laughed again, as if at himself. 'Where they do be from, they never see the likes of a water tank.'

He'd been away himself and once he'd tried to enlist in the army but they wouldn't take him. When he was young he'd fallen and damaged his knee down at Kilronan harbour. He went in to Galway but you had to be 100 per cent fit. He knew the wider world, however. He'd lived in Birmingham (told me the house number and street where he lived) and he'd worked at the Isle of Grain. He'd been a fisherman, taking Yanks out fishing too, and now he was a jarvey, which is what you do as you get older. I told him how once or twice I'd tottered the low road home, the worse for wear from Guinness.

'Ah sure,' he smiled, 'didn't we all, so no one could see us, staggering and falling over? I see the likes of them doing it now, you know, the young fellas.'

He named them and laughed at the thought. And then he showed me the seals off the shore below Mainistir, waiting, as he said, for the tide to ebb a little more before they'd come ashore to perch. He was very eager that I should see the seals. He identified birds for me and I got a glimpse of how much the natural world was second nature to him to know. So that was what became of the fighting man, after all: now in round sixty-three and up against age (who always punches above his weight and goes the distance).

Now the sand raced through the little hourglass for me. I found another message from Michael and yet managed to miss him again. But as I stepped out next morning, at eight o'clock, due to sail for Rossaveal at nine, down he came, rattling in his red van, and stopped and came up to me and greeted me warmly. A barrel-chested man he had become but I could still see the youth in him I'd once known, always full of laughter. How many years my junior? Only seven or eight, but at that time just those few years seem far more. Now, as I understood, he skippered his own boat, up and down from Galway, in and out of Killybegs.

There was a great deal of activity in Kilronan that morning.

Michael told me why. All the fishing boats currently in the harbour were preparing to sail out to the bar of the island. They were to form a reception party to greet the first new trawler to join the island fleet for longer than anyone could remember. Surely not since the *Ard Aengus*? Wrecked in '68? I wondered aloud, lost in my time-warp. But no one could remember her. Everyone was in it now, as Michael said, and the place was humming. The fishermen and jarvies were on their mobiles, chattering like yuppies in Galway. To whom? To each other? Out went the escort to the east and, as it sailed, the morning, suitably, became dramatically grey and cold. The boats shrank almost from sight into the new day's narrow light but at last crossed broadside on, passing behind Straw Island. Then there she loomed, the *Shauna Ann*, proud property of Mr Fitzpatrick of Killeany. (So I think I heard say.)

'Give her a week,' said Michael, ungrudgingly, 'and she'll be just like the others.'

Flares shot in arcs across her as she turned and headed in. The other boats followed in procession, led by the lifeboat. As she neared, you could see her brilliant red paintwork and what I took to be her great deepwater bulk. But Michael advised me she wasn't a big boat compared with some of them, not at all. Some of them were crewed by as many as fifty men. Her owner and what I took to be his sons, as well as many others, were all aboard, waving to their womenfolk and children. As she neared, the minibus jarvies blew their horns and the women shrieked and shrilled. The other boats, including the *Draoicht na Farraige*, blew what they had to blow. It was a kind of blessing, and made me think what such a blessing might seek to forfend. Michael had spoken to me of being of the party that had searched and searched the

Sound to find any sign of the *Lively Lady*. She went down in '82, a forty-footer and too slight a vessel to contend with the storm that ran there. So Mikey McDonough and Brian O'Flaherty perished with her. Think of their last gasp and sight of day in bleak North Sound. 'He always said that was how he would die,' said Padraig of Mikey McDonough.

But now the *Draoicht na Farraige* strained to be off, and so as suddenly as that last time on the *Naomh Eanna*, my time imploded, and soon the last sight of the island vanished again between the sky and sea.

I thought that I had come full circle. I thought the story of my going back, just three days, brief and sketchy, had found a fitting close, one to open that world for me again, and bring it from the past for ever, freeing me of it all at last. But there was yet another, unforeseeable circle to be drawn.

I had some Lilliputian business to attend to in Dublin. So I stopped over, staying in Amiens Street (at the Old Dubliner). Then on the morning I was due to sail, once more to Liverpool, I decided I'd walk to the terminal down the Liffey in the morning. I still like, as much as ever I did when younger, the uplifting prospect of a harbour and a sea-road. But soon I found myself lost in an impenetrable maze of wharves and warehouses, basins and quays. There seemed to me to be no way through. To make matters worse, it was a warm morning too, warm for wearing a rucksack on your back, heavy with a week's wear and reading. Now in some desperation, trying again and again to get through, I turned this way and that. If there was a passage through the maze, I couldn't find it. The time ticked by, as it seemed, faster and faster. I was in danger of missing my sailing. I realized I'd no choice but to walk all the way back into Dublin, to find a last-ditch taxi. I began to despair as I walked, now half at a run, my habitual folly threatening to thwart me again.

Then, suddenly, as I rounded a corner, beside a rundown warehouse, I looked across the quay to my left and saw, in the far corner, unmistakable to my eye, even after more than thirty years, the *Naomh Eanna* herself. Would you believe? There she was, moored up, rusting, listing, some blue bunting in her rigging. I could not and could only believe my eyes. It was the *Naomh Eanna*, I knew from just her outline. I didn't need to see her name. I knew her so well. My eye had kept its youth. I had my camera with me, to record the evidence, but my camera had no film in. I lingered looking after her, across the dank basin. But I couldn't reach her, and I couldn't stay. Just so you might leave your love, your family, friends and relations, for ever in some heart-wrung, lingering harbourside farewell. As I turned away from her, I saw a man parked in a van and crossed to ask him did he know what place this was?

'Charlotte Quay,' he said, 'Charlotte.'

So there the two of us met again and my mind flooded with enough memories to float her off, and myself with her, out of the lightweight Dublin breeze that clacked and rattled in her lame rigging, and out to the west. The sudden sight of her, after all that time, made me feel, as any foolish fatalist might, that the gods had written my story for me, and brought it round full circle now, not by any accident, but by design.

MAY, SEPTEMBER 2000